CELEBRITY
SERVICE
BY GEOFF RAMM

Celebrity Service (2nd edition)

First edition published by CreateSpace Independent Publishing 2015

This edition published 2018 by SRA Books

www.geofframm.com

ISBN: 978-1-912300-18-1

Design | Layout | Graphics | Publishing Jedi : Mark Moore, Purely Mint Promotions

Graphic Illustrations: Ian West

Editor-in-chief: Dr Emma Sutton

RAVING REVIEWS

"Even if you think you offer 5-star service, there is always room for improvement and this easy-to-read book will help transform your customer service ethos. Geoff through some great real-world examples is quite rightly challenging us to identify our competitive service gap and improve customer service to 'celebrity' status which will benefit the top and bottom line."

Phillip Singh – Vice President – EMEA

"Geoff Ramm has done it again. His OMG marketing approach really helped me to change my view of how I promote my business a few years ago, and now his CELEBRITY service idea has just raised the bar again. A simple, elegant idea that everyone in your team will instantly understand, yet profound enough to impact your business strategy, Geoff delivers an important message in a punchy package. Highly recommended. It's already made a difference to the way I approach my customers."

Dr Graeme Codrington – Co-founder and International director – TomorrowToday

"Hello. This is your business wake-up call and Geoff Ramm is here to kick-start the action. Celebrity Service is a relevant, refreshing and witty read that could help take your service to another level. Do yourself a favour and put it at the top of your list. (Or go one step better and get Geoff to present to your team – it will be a session to remember!)"

Sharmila Nahna – Chief of Relationships – Ovations International

"Geoff knows how to capture an audience, whether it's during his interactive keynotes or through his books. He always delivers powerful, practical examples that are sure to inspire audiences to help them stand out from the competition through excellent marketing and service. Celebrity Service is a must read, it demonstrates how great service can stop you in your tracks anywhere in the world. The question you will be asking yourself after reading this is... how do I measure up?"

Natalie Hudson – Marketing & Membership Manager – VENUEMASTERS

"What I love about Geoff's work is that while everyone else is busy coming up with the latest interesting idea, Geoff has always moved on past that to the most difficult business of actually applying it and making it real in your business. Like OMG the ideas in this book are applicable to pretty much any business. They are based on an easily understandable but revolutionary concept and, if implemented, will transform your business... and indeed the world. Imagine an entire economy based on the idea of giving everyone in it Celebrity Service! Geoff is without doubt the funniest, most down-to-earth and most practical speaker and writer in customer service today. I urge you to buy this book and listen to the man speak!"

Caspar Berry – Motivational Speaker

"At last a book focused on the true meaning of outstanding service. A great read and one that highlights that exceptional customer service is not dead. I have read many books about how to get the best out of customer-facing employees, but nothing provides such excellent referencing, true real-life examples and a humorous relevant twist."

James Foice – Managing Director – ASAP

"Geoff Ramm proves that customer service is not a complex conundrum of convoluted issues requiring a cadre of committees to correct. Instead he brilliantly opens your eyes to a new perspective that gives way to a simpler solution that leads to amazing customer service."

Dawnna St Louis – Professional Speaker & Author

"What an absolute delight to read, Geoff's style is so brilliantly executed that you can instantly visualise the scene and better still you're transported there, hanging on the words, waiting to see what's happened. More than that though, is the use of examples which are things everyone can relate to and not the stock standard 'safe' brands other people use when talking about marketing and customer service. Each example is brought to life with a real element of human brilliance. I found myself nodding as I read the pages, even laughing out loud, knowing I've been in situations like this or seen things like this happen! The Celebrity Service examples can't fail to make you smile, and leave me wondering how I can usurp my customers' expectations!"

Lissa Balmer – International Trade Advisor – UKTI

YOU PROBABLY THINK YOU DELIVER GREAT SERVICE.

BUT THEN A CELEBRITY WALKED IN... AND EVERYTHING CHANGED!

GEOFF RAMM, CELEBRITY SERVICE SPEAKER

FOOTBALL IS SO...
OF PRETENDING
YOU'RE HU...
RUGBY IS A...

foot print...
behind may fa...
but in your heart t...
will always stay

Check your
Cabin Luggage Here

THE
BOOK SMITH

THIS
FACILITY
IS FOR USE BY
OUR FOUR
LEGGED FRIENDS

PLEASE QUENCH
YOUR THIRST WITH
OUR BEST WISHES
VIRGIN TRAINS

WHO IS GEOFF?

Like you, Geoff Ramm, the creator and author of Celebrity Service and OMG Marketing, knows the only way you can attract more customers is to create jaw-dropping marketing.

Not only that but great customer service leads to lucrative, repeat business.

So how do you create a customer experience that has you talked about for decades to come, and has your customers queuing overnight for more?

Geoff knows the Jedi Mind Trick to make you craved by your customers, envied by your competitors and raved about in your industry.

In his interactive keynote presentations, your delegates and teams will not only discover out-of-this-world ideas, they will come up with them and be excited to implement them too.

Within this his second book, Geoff will reveal the philosophy, the stories and the award-winning results which have led companies across six continents to out-perform their competitors.

Geoff was born in South Shields, is married to Hayley and dad to Grace and Elliot.

He loves pizza, cider and for his sins supports Sunderland AFC.

FOREWORD

The subject of customer service or, customer experience as it is increasingly known, has been the subject of numerous books over the years, many of which I have bought, several of which I have actually read!

They range from the enduring classics by the likes of Ken Blanchard to complex body language analysis, Neuro-Linguistic Programming and psychological mapping of behaviour. Often these books are intellectually engaging and thought provoking, but the concepts they describe can be very difficult to execute across the frontline of an organisation. That's not because staff on the frontline can't understand the concepts. It's because in successful organisations staff on the frontline are usually too busy and distracted to spend time working out how to apply them – too busy serving customers!

By contrast this is a simple book, written in simple language that makes it easy to read and central to the book is a simple concept that is easy to grasp. In all my years at John Lewis and with the many organisations I have consulted for since, the simple ideas were, almost exclusively, the most effective.

The idea of Celebrity Service taps into a dominant and growing culture that has been in existence since the beginning of the last century and continues to grow annually – just look at the reality TV programmes: X Factor, Britain's Got Talent, The Voice and, of course, in business, The Apprentice. Everyone can immediately identify with how they might treat their favourite celebrity and how that may currently be different from how they treat their day-to-day customers.

Couple a simple but effective concept with some wonderful illustrative stories, and Geoff is a great storyteller, and you have a book that could make a real difference to your organisation. I hope you enjoy reading it as much as I did.

Andrew McMillan – Former National Customer Service Manager, John Lewis Principal at Engaging Service • www.engagingservice.com

CONTENTS

*To the people who put a
smile on every customer's face,
I thank you.
Your service will never
go unnoticed...*

Dedicated to Hayley, Grace & Elliot x

*"The Queen thinks the
world smells of paint."*

Billy Connolly

ALSO
AVAILABLE

OBSERVATIONAL
MARKETING
GREATS

BORN
OUT OF
FRUSTRATION

My love and passion for marketing is well-documented in my first book, OMG (Observational Marketing Greats), and although as a child I remember great marketing, I must confess I can't recall the first time I received great customer service. So at what age do we start to remember customer service?

I believe it's when you start to earn your own money and take home that first pay packet. With that hard-earned money in your pocket, you now have the ability to choose where you spend it. As you hand over your cash, you're entering into a transaction which comes with a series of expectations – you pay for your purchase from the vendor, and in return you expect a great product, a smooth process, and excellent service. Maybe it's because you are wiser to what is going on, or maybe when you start making your own way in life you appreciate how much you've had to work to be able to afford cars, holidays, clothes and groceries, but by this stage I think what we all expect, as a bare minimum, is good service.

As a business you may not be able to fight your way to number one on Google; you may never be able to compete with large-scale advertising campaigns; you may never reach the dizzy heights of a social media viral sensation, but there is one thing you can always compete for (and win) – the hearts and minds of your clients and customers.

The only way to achieve this is through outstanding customer service. In an ever-changing business world where competition comes from online, the high street, overseas, and no doubt in the future outer space, this is the one true competitive differentiating factor for you and your team.

So why is it that as a husband, a dad, a businessman, and a professional speaker, I am becoming increasingly frustrated by poor service? What disappoints me more than anything are the barriers, the rules, the red tape, and the sheer doggedness that stops me, you, and many others from being happy with the service we are receiving.

The longer I am a customer, the more I notice a frequent unwillingness to delight. Surely this should never be the case!

There are countless books, manuals, training courses, customer service gurus, online and on-the-shelf resources just waiting to be explored, digested and used, but how many of these ideas and service concepts are taken on-board and willingly delivered?

I am known for my Observational take on the marketing world, but for many years I have also observed the world of customer service with a magnifying glass and fine-toothed comb. While half of my business is focused on helping businesses and audiences gain more clients, the other half is concentrated on helping businesses to upgrade their customer service beyond that of the competition – to become memorable for all the right reasons.

So, it is with my Observational eye that I am bringing to the fore a different way of helping you to look at your service; a way in which you, your team, and your business can improve every conceivable customer touchpoint in your organisation.

People kill brands, people kill service, and people have the power to break or make your reputation. NB: For "people" see: team, partner, cleaner, maid, chauffeur, receptionist, call centre, distribution, driver and, yes… YOU!

Poor service delivered by anyone in your company gives your customers fuel to ignite a flame with the potential to destroy your business. You have been warned!

There are hundreds of books on customer service, focusing on what you – the CEO, director, executive, business owner or entrepreneur – can do to revolutionise your team, organisation or business. Flick through the pages and you may recognise some of these phrases; give yourself a gold star if you do…

Delight your customer! Go the extra mile! Exceed expectations! Treat the customer how you wish to be treated!

Sound good? Sound familiar? It all sounds rather bland and same-old, same-old for my liking. This is the sort of material I read back in university and college. What does it really mean? If you were to repeat these mundane phrases to your team, would they really be inspired to make the difference?

Is this it? Is this the answer to incredible word-of-mouth reputation building? Is this the answer that leads to customers beating down your door and queuing overnight to get in?

No, which is why I've become increasingly frustrated.

For all the CRM software and data developments, there has never been a seismic shift in how customers are served. We're simply not using the information available to us to come up with creative ways to out-smart and out-serve the competition.

So, the time has come to say "enough is enough". It is time to think differently. It is time to inspire your team with a new outlook, a new vision, and a work environment where common sense and independent thought are at the heart of decision-making. The aim is to improve each and every customer touchpoint and service experience at every opportunity.

If you've come here expecting chapter and verse in service psychology, you will be deeply disappointed. However, if you are looking for **ONE BIG IDEA** to invigorate you and everyone around your business to think differently and to find the gap your competition can't touch, this book is full of suggestions to inspire it! There is no guarantee, but this one book may just hold the answer to propel you to your competitive edge, and the answer may well be easier than you think.

There is a new way of customer service thinking and, like Father Christmas on the 24th December, it's exciting, it's full of surprises, and it's on its way to be delivered by your business.

PLEASE DO
NOT
READ

(it will only make you angry...)

The immortal line... "Don't make me angry, you won't like me when I am angry" came from the lips of Dr David Banner when sheer frustration would turn to anger, and then into rage, and within minutes a mountainous green creature would emerge, swiftly followed by a visit to the tailor's.

**The stories you are about to read are 100% true.
Every one of them had me turning green – not with envy,
but with a Hulkesque rage!**

FIRST JOB: YOU'VE BEEN WARNED

Having graduated from Sunderland University Business School, I spent over a year posting CVs (yes, it was a while ago now) trying to plant my first foot on a career ladder with the name marketing attached to it. In between sending CVs and speaking to recruitment agencies, I had to take a job to help contribute to the mortgage and bills, so I manned the telephones of a gas and electric utility company.

I won't go into too much detail, but hasten to add that we were one of the darlings on the BBC's Watchdog programme most weeks, with a reputation for underhand sales and service techniques. It was during this time that the gas and electricity markets were de-regulated and it seemed that some salespeople were going out of their way to sign up anyone they could, by any means necessary, in order to grab that all-important commission.

Unsuspecting customers would receive a letter on their mat explaining that they were going to be leaving their current supplier, and would very soon be switching over to us! You could imagine the emotion of the callers when they rang to complain (and rightly so). Irate customers demanding to stay with their current supplier and not to be switched.

Sadly, we had to tell them that it was too far into the system and that this switch was going to happen, regardless. An awful job, an awful way to treat customers, and a sharp welcome to start my career in the big world of real work.

I don't remember her name, but I do remember an elderly lady in tears on the telephone saying she didn't want to switch, and that she must have been duped at the doorstep.

She was in such a state, and I tried everything I could to help calm her down and to help her, but a few taps on the keyboard confirmed my fears – she was coming to us, regardless. I said to her that I'd call her back and would do my best to stop this from happening. Her reply: "Will it be this week?"

"It will be in the next hour," I said.

She didn't believe me, so I gave her my personal extension and told her to ring me at any time. I rang back within the hour and told her the bad news. She'd stopped crying by now, and then completely shocked me… "For all your help and honesty in calling me back I will stay with you… can I keep your number?"

From an old-aged pensioner crying down the phone, to someone who was now happy to stay – I was both amazed and delighted.

Of course, all incoming and outgoing numbers and calls are monitored, and the following day I was called into the Manager's office. I was looking forward to telling her what had happened and the amazing customer u-turn the day before, but before I could speak I was receiving my very first, and ultimately last, verbal warning. The reason? For giving out my extension number; a move which was against company policy and The Rules.

It was at this point that the essence of this company's customer service hit home. It simply did not exist. Being nice or, indeed, doing the right thing to make a customer happy was behaviour that merited punishment and reprimand. What more can I say?

One week later, I left… I had found the first rung on my career ladder marked **"Marketing"**.

THE HUSBAND: HANGING ON AT THE END OF THE WEDDING

We hired the photographer, videographer, the cars, venue, bought the favours, flowers, and everything else you could imagine. We hired the menswear and bridesmaids' dresses, but bought the dress – please remember – we bought the dress.

The day after the big day we were off on our honeymoon, so I asked my parents if they could take the hired clothes back to the bridal shop to reclaim the deposit. We returned from honeymoon to find that all of the hire clothes were actually still at home. I rang my parents to see if everything was alright, and they explained that they had returned everything, as we had requested, to the bridal shop, but they had been told the deposit couldn't be returned due to a missing clothes hanger.

When they had taken the clothes back, the shop assistant behind the counter was making wedding small talk and had asked for the bridal dress clothes hanger. The hanger was not there. The hanger for the dress – that we had bought, remember – was not there! The upshot to this minor incident was that we could not get the money back until the shop had the clothes hanger back in their possession.

We hunted high and low, but, with all the upheaval of the wedding, we could not find it. Eventually we gave up the search, went back to apologise, told them we could not find it, and finally – very begrudgingly – we got our deposit back. We had spent a small fortune with that business, and this minor detail spoiled the entire experience which had, up to this point, been brilliant.

Years later we moved house and, as we were moving boxes… we found it.

Now I know what you are thinking – the hanger must have been gold plated? Laden with diamantes? Or perhaps diamond encrusted? Not quite. To see this exquisite work of art for yourself, turn to page 130. Once you've picked yourself back up off the floor, come back here…

Our photographer for the day was very good; a bit pricey, but good, and umpteen albums were purchased by our families after the big day. Years later, we received a letter from him saying that "Due to their growing success, they have too many negatives taking up too much room and are therefore going to have to throw them away to free up some space". Rather than pop them in the same envelope and say, "but we thought you'd like them at no cost," the letter continued with: "If you would like them before we bin them they are available to you for an amazing £50 extra."

We were the first of our close friends to get married. We spent months researching venues, visiting suppliers, and emptying the bank account to find the so-called best-of-the-best for our big day. Naturally, when the time came for some of our friends to be married, they often asked us for our recommendations. We gladly gave them, but not for the photographer, and not for the bridal shop.

People who put rules and greed before putting a smile on your face will puncture their business until it becomes flat. The customer who you've served poorly will never recommend you, but will undoubtedly talk about the negative experience they had with you.

MERCURY RISING

A few years later, on the 1st March 2002, I started up my own business called Mercury Marketing. Like all sensible people, I did a bit of research before I launched.

I took to the phones, pretending to be a member of my target clientele – entrepreneurs and small-to-medium enterprises – calling to ask marketing companies what services they offered, how much they charged, etc. (I must warn you that this was pre-Google, and some readers may find the following sentence alien or somewhat disturbing.) I reached for the Yellow Pages, and contacted every marketing company in the region… there were 11 in total.

The following results have been ingrained in my mind since 2002…

- Three companies simply rang out, with no answer machine.
- Three said they did not market entrepreneurs/SMEs (two actually laughed, thinking it was beneath them).
- Two companies said they would ring me back (I am still waiting, but as the eternal optimist, I am sure it will be any day now).
- Two said they would send some information. (Like an excitable puppy, I am still looking out for the postman with a packet from one company. The other did appear, but the quality of the materials and print was truly awful… homemade, at best.)
- One said he was writing a book on marketing and, when it was available, I should buy it!

So here I am posing as a potential client, and not one person helped, advised or encouraged. However frustrated I felt at the time, I was equally happy that this was the competition I was about to face…

Game On.

THE COUPLE: WHEN JIM BOWEN MET GOLDILOCKS

Way back in the 1980s there was a hugely popular trivia gameshow on UK television called Bullseye, hosted by Jim Bowen. A mixture of the pub game/sport of darts and general knowledge, it was a show that spawned many a catchphrase, but one in particular was "Look at what you could have won". This was frequently said to the losing couple at the finale of the show if they had failed to score 101 or more with their 6 darts. The curtain would open to reveal a fitted kitchen, a Vauxhall Nova or, more likely, a speedboat!

Some years ago we spent the weekend in Stirling, right in the heart of Scotland – a beautiful place, rich with William Wallace history. We left our hotel room at a well-known hotel chain, had breakfast, and took an early morning stroll. When we came back we walked towards our room and could see a chink of light at the end of the corridor.

"The cleaners must be in there already," I said. We walked in and there on the bed was the cleaner... asleep (aka Goldilocks)!

I walked gingerly in and quietly said, "Hello?" Nothing; she was flat out.

"Hello?" I said, a little louder now. On the third, much louder attempt, she awoke, startled. She shot up out of bed, brushed herself down, and started to clean the room.

We said, "It's okay, the room is clean," and asked her to leave.

We spent the next 24 hours in shock.

Sleeping in our bed like Goldilocks was only half the story, so where does Jim Bowen fit in? We came back later that day and decided we needed to inform the management, not wanting to get the girl into trouble, but they needed to know what happened. They thanked us for telling them. 24 hours later we finished breakfast – ironically with porridge – and checked out. On checking out the manager said, "Thanks for letting us know, and we are really sorry for what happened yesterday". He foolishly continued, "It's a shame you complained later in the day as we could have given you last night for FREE, but the computer says we can't now."

Look at what you could have won!

In the most stupid of stupid circumstances, we were at fault for complaining "too late", and the manager did not have the authorisation or common sense to override the computer.

Is there anything more frustrating than knowing a computer is ruling your decisions, regardless of what is right or wrong?!

THE DAD: SITTING ON THE FENCE?

Two panels of our fence came down due to high winds, making the back garden far too dangerous for our two young children to play in. With two less than impressed kids, we had to act fast.

Calling on recommendations from friends and a few firms from a local magazine (the one they paid to be in to attract work!), appointments were made over the phone to measure up and to then provide a quote.

One company never sent the quote as promised.

The company we chose, decided not to call us back to start the work.

Our second choice arrived a week late and took two weeks longer than expected (as they had double booked the diary).

Is this it? In one of the biggest global recessions ever recorded, I can only assume that the stories in the Press are nothing but a smokescreen/media hype, as it appears no one who we called needed the business.

TERRIBLE TWOS

"Wait until you reach the terrible twos" is a phrase often wheeled out by friends and family to strike fear into the minds of unsuspecting parents of babies. Tempers, tantrums and refusing just about everything are the general rules of thumb. But no, this is not about Elliot, who had just turned two; this is about two companies who believe being awkward, stubborn and irritable is the correct way to behave.

For his birthday, we bought Elliot a combined wooden seat and sand pit. It arrived from the online store in time for Mr MacGyver Ramm to assemble it. After two hours of building and, like a blast from the 1980s furniture past, there was a screw missing – one that would ensure the structure was safe to play on.

Disappointed at 20:45pm? Yes! But fear not, I went online to this rather large and famous brand and emailed customer services using their online form (particularly mentioning the fact that I needed a replacement fixing in time for Elliot's birthday). There was no response the following day so I rang up...

The response...

"Oh, sorry. We can't send you out a replacement part. Although this product is ours, you purchased it from (think of the largest toy retailer and you probably have the name), so you need to contact them."

So I did.

The response…

"Ah, we can't open another box and send you this part. However, it's a generic fixing so I would advise you to go to your local DIY shop, purchase one and we'll refund you for the fixing."

So I did.

Two large DIY chain stores and one independent shop later… "Sorry, this is a specific part for the product; you'll need to speak to them."

So I did.

"Oh, unfortunately, this product is now sold out. The best we can do is to order the part for you from…" wait for it… "POLAND".

The first email was sent in May 2014 and at that time they said they would order the part and post it to me. Even now, in 2018, I have yet to receive a response. When I rang back for the final time, the customer services person read back all of the previous conversations and the promises they had made, but still didn't offer a solution.

I also took to Twitter to report the service and seek help – zero response!

I live in hope that one day this elusive fixing will arrive.

Feel free to email me at geoff@geofframm.com for a screw update and I'll tell you if it ever arrived.

To celebrate Elliot's birthday, we decided to take him to a theme park which has a famous toy brand attached to it (we thought it would be better than a half-built sand pit). The plan was to book a themed bedroom (months in advance) so that on the morning of his birthday he'd wake up to toys, cake and balloons.

We travelled four hours by car and duly arrived at the check-in desk, and couldn't wait to see the looks on Grace and Elliot's faces, as we'd kept this a secret surprise for them.

"Good afternoon, Mr Ramm..."

"Good afternoon."

"Ah, has no one contacted you?"

"No. Should they have?"

"There is a problem with your themed room. You can't have it."

"Okay. So can we have another themed room, please?"

"No, they're all booked."

At this point I let off more steam than the hotel could carry!

"What we can do is put you in a standard room at a reduced rate."

Insert a barrage of discontent with the reception staff holding their ground, a manageress who had left and could not be contacted, and knowledge that the secret surprise was ruined. I was fuming.

For over 45 minutes we exchanged our views and we had to stand our own ground to get the very best out of the problem. We settled on an upgraded room that night, and had a great day in the park the next day. Having eventually spoken to the manageress the next morning, we stayed for an unplanned second night in the themed room and really did have a great time.

So what could have been done differently?

They should have called us!

They should have looked at the "Any Other Requirements" box (are these boxes meant to be ignored?) that said this trip was for a child's birthday.

They should have made suggestions other than a downgrade.

They should have apologised! And what was the problem with the room we had booked?

The electronic locks on the doors had broken.

Can we go back to things called "Keys"?

When the football, rugby or cricket team is on a poor run, the boss, manager or coach will stop and go back to basics – running, passing, shooting, catching. Get the basics right and you are on your way.

Business is just the same. Keep your customer updated at all times, have a better response than anticipated, and stick to what works.

All of these examples could have been avoided with simple common sense.

After every example I asked myself one question… What if?

What if I were someone deemed more important – would I have got the deposit back without the hanger, first time?

What if I were deemed more important – would I have received the photograph negatives for free?

What if I were deemed more important – would Goldilocks have stayed out of our bed, and would we have got the second night free in the hotel?

What if I were deemed more important – would the fence have been quoted for and repaired on time?

What if Elliot was the son of someone more important – would he have been in his themed bedroom and had a complete, safe toy on his birthday after a new fixing had been delivered on time?

If only I, we, us, were more important.

COME IN NUMBER 10

YOUR TIME IS UP!

On a scale of 1 to 10, how would you rate your overall customer service right now? (1 being truly awful, 10 being incredibly amazing.)

If you marked yourself 1–4, you know you have an awful lot of work to do; if you are 5–8, then you know you could be doing better. Even if you are confident enough to choose a 9 or a 10, I know you can easily improve every aspect of your service further.

Many scales end with 10 (10 being the highest mark possible) but are there numbers beyond this for you, your team, and your business?

You see, we all believe we are delivering constantly high levels of service, but what I am about to reveal is the game changer. It will shift your entire mindset to how you deliver service in future.

WHY CELEBRITY? WHY NOT ★★★★★ SERVICE?

Five star has always been the pinnacle of service standards, but what if you or I were to visit a 5-star establishment and receive 5-star service and then a celebrity walked in – there would, again, be a difference in attitude, delivery and persona.

The world famous 7-star hotel, the Burj Al Arab in Dubai, shows clearly how five stars, just like any number, can always be superseded.

It's widely known that a celebrity does not have to do much to be offered the best seat in the house or secure the best table in an already full restaurant.

Celebrity is greater than five star. It top trumps its status. It is reserved only for royalty and Hollywood A-listers. It was probably best summed up in 1990 when Miss Vivian Ward entered a Hollywood boutique and was shown the door moments later, due to her inappropriate dress at the time. Oscar nominee, Julia Roberts, played the part of Miss Ward in *Pretty Woman*. For those of you who haven't seen the movie, she walked into the same store a day later wearing a more conservative, expensive outfit and uttered the lines: "Big mistake. Big. Huge," and swiftly left the store, leaving the sales assistants wishing they had provided Celebrity Service to all their customers.

Of course this is just Hollywood, right? Wrong! Before launching my own business in 2002 I was a marketing manager of a motor retail group in the UK, marketing and promoting some of the world's most iconic brands: Honda, Chrysler and Toyota, to name just a few. My main objective was simple – to encourage you to take a test drive. A salesperson would then take over with the aim of converting the sale.

Our good friends were in the market for a new car, a sporty two-seater. I made them aware of the new Toyota we had at our Durham branch and told them it was ready for a test drive. They went to the branch that Sunday morning.

When I next spoke to them I was delighted to hear that they had purchased their brand-new sports car and it was going to be delivered in one month's time. But, they didn't buy if from our dealer! They drove a further 30 miles to another garage and purchased the new car from them!

What the...?!

When they had arrived in Durham they asked to test drive the car, but the salesperson said that wouldn't be possible. The dealership was tight on space, so numerous cars would need to have been moved and, as the salesperson was short on time, energy and colleagues that morning, he said that they could not test drive it that day but to come back soon.

I was furious. One person's lack of service led to the main competitor securing a great sale. Big mistake. Big. Huge.

WELCOME TO THE BIRTH OF CELEBRITY SERVICE

It's not something I sat down, thought long and hard about, or created; in fact, the term Celebrity Service appeared out of nowhere during a talk I did at a conference in the UK some years ago.

This half-day event was split into two. The first half was all about marketing ideas and how businesses could gain customers and clients by standing out from the competition. There was a short coffee and comfort break and the second half featured a host of customer service ideas and stories on how to retain customers.

As the MC introduced me back onto stage, for some reason I completely changed my planned opening line, and said: "Do you treat all of your customers in the same way?" In an audience of around 300 people, roughly half of the room nodded their heads, apart from one woman who was sat near the front. She shouted out, "Absolutely, Geoff!" I was taken aback – as was the rest of the audience; she was so adamant and so animated. I replied, "Wonderful. You treat every customer with the same high level of standards each and every day, no matter what?"

"Yes," came the answer.

"What sort of business do you have?"

"I run a boutique store selling children's toys, homeware and kitchenware, all made out of wood, metal and stone. It's very exclusive and rather expensive."

"This sounds great. Now give me examples of how you deliver great service all of the time?"

"We serve tea and coffee."

"Wow, how much?"

"It's complimentary."

"What else do you do?"

"We have comfy chairs in the store so people can sit and browse before buying."

And then I paused… And from nowhere asked her the question that was about to change everything.

"Okay, but what if a celebrity were to walk into your store tomorrow?"

"Like who?" she replied.

I was caught on the hop! So said, "Do you like men or women?"

"Men."

"Okay, think of an A-list… Celebrity… Hollywood… Male… Movie… Hunk…"

She thought for a few moments (with a wry smile on her face) and then shouted out two answers…

"George and Brad." (You know how hunky you are when you don't need a surname!)

"So, picture the scene, George Clooney is making a movie in this area. He's been here for six months and is flying back to the United States tomorrow, but before he goes he wants to buy some gifts for his family. He's heard all about you and your store and wants to come in and buy. However, he's tired. He's tired of the paparazzi and tired of signing autographs. So he phones you up and says…

"'Hi there, I'm George Clooney, I want to come to your store tomorrow but I'd love to have some privacy away from autograph hunters and paparazzi. Would you mind closing the store for me, please?'"

So I asked this lady sat at the front of the audience, "Would you close it for George?"

"Oh yes," came the reply with an ever widening smile.

"Great. Now I am staying here tonight and I am speaking at another event tomorrow. Would you close the shop for me?"

She remained silent and ever so slowly shook her head from side to side…

Cue 299 people raising their eyebrows and in a split second one embarrassed lady put her hand over her mouth and let out a gasp, "Ooh… I would treat customers differently."

"That's okay. I would expect that, but, what else would you do for George tomorrow morning?"

At this point most of the audience laughed. The lady thought about it and to everyone's amazement, including mine, she came up with half a dozen ideas in just 30 seconds!

These were the answers I can recall from that day:

"I'd get my hair done." (She mentioned her sister was a stylist.)

"I'd wear my best dress."

"The wooden floor has needed varnishing for at least six months – I'd do it tonight." (See Billy Connolly quote on page 15.)

And the last idea was the real shocker...

"I'd get rid of the tea and coffee."

"What?!"

"Yes, but I'd bring in proper coffee."

Half a dozen ideas in 30 seconds, based on a celebrity hypothetically entering her business. She said she was already delivering the highest possible service, and then a celebrity walked in... and changed everything about her attitude and mindset on service.

Quite simply, there is a gap in your customer service you never knew existed and Celebrity Service will stretch that gap to leave your competitors in its wake.

(As illustrated by a recent audience member in her business...)

CELEBRITY

SERVICE

Thank you Geoff!

'BRAD PITT' SERVICE

this is the tool for me to communicate my vision!

STANDARD 'EXCELLENT' SERVICE

BUILDING THE FOUNDATIONS

OF A CELEBRITY SERVICE CULTURE

HAPPY TEAM + HAPPIER CUSTOMERS = REPEAT BUSINESS

WARNING:

THE FOLLOWING COMPANIES WILL MAKE YOU WANT TO UPDATE
YOUR CV AND APPLY TO WORK WITH THEM. FOREVER.

We often hear of the coolest brands and places to work – you know, the funky design types of Google, Lego & Facebook. But what I am about to reveal "for your eyes only" is the greatest employee focused business I've ever walked into.

Have you ever watched the Jim Carey classic, *The Truman Show*? You know the one where he wakes up everyday and everyone around him is happy, smiling and glad to be alive! It's fake, right? Yes, of course it is. It's all a part of the reality TV show. Well, if you ever have the chance to visit a certain business near Wrexham in North Wales, you will come across the Welsh Truman Show. Everyone there is happy, smiley and bubbly! But why? One of the reasons may be due to the fact that the management asked every staff member as they were planning their brand-new office design, "What would you like to see in your new workplace?"

And here is what I found...

Moneypenny (OMG is this the greatest name ever for a PA business?) has 500 of the happiest PAs answering calls from many of the world's leading brands, as well as entrepreneurial businesses.

As you "only live twice", I decided to go down a day early to have a guided tour of their purpose-built headquarters.

As you walk into the lobby area on the wall to your left are hundreds of names of the individuals who have worked and still are working there. On the right-hand side wall are the staff members who have been there for a decade. In life we honour the fallen with their names on a wall but here at Moneypenny they highlight and showcase the people who have all helped to make them such a success – a great touch.

> Thank you
> to this extraordinary team
> who made Moneypenny
> what it is today,
> and to those who will add
> more tomorrow - by
> doing amazing things for
> our wonderful clients.
>
> 1ST JULY 2016

When I signed in I met Lynne. You'll not find a friendlier front-of-house person. She was Moneypenny's very first employee. She asked if I'd like a drink. Now forget about kettles and machines – if you want a flat white, cappaccino or latte, simply make your choice on the iPad device and it will instantly pour. A great user experience. And above us, whilst the cup was filling up, we were shadowed by a giant treehouse which housed a really cool meeting space.

EVEN THE TEXT ON THE CUP IS POSITIVE!

And then there are the toilets. The staff asked for something more homely and less like an office cubicle. So the doors are designed as front doors you'd find in your own street.

And there's more. One thing I really loved was the Mojo Wall featuring many of the wonderful customer services experiences the PAs had delivered for clients – these weren't just Post-its on a cork board – these were designed, printed and expertly presented, taking pride of place in the building.

Beth Roberts got her Mojo for going the extra mile and making a client's visit extra special with cakes and their own goody bag.

DECEMBER 2015

Ashleigh got her Mojo for sending her client's wife a birthday card just because it was a nice thing to do

APRIL 2011

Walking past the raised seating area and out onto the balcony there were picnic tables and chairs and rugs to keep you warm should you wish to sit out and overlook the garden. But wait for the next bit...

Immediately below us was a pub! That's right. You read that right. A pub. It's called the Dog & Bone (rhyming slang for telephone). With table football, TV screens, table tennis (sadly, no Casino Royale) and, of course, a well-stocked bar. The bar is run by volunteer employees at pretty much cost price for everyone. Wow. It was in the pub where I delivered my session the next day.

Celebrity Service starts at home, it starts with your team, it begins with your fellow colleagues. Get this right and the challenge of delivering a greater service and experience for your clients and customers becomes an awful lot easier.

Are your team members the happiest they can be?

What can you ask them to help transform your place of work?

BABY SLIDE

Welcome to an organisation packed with the most creative and passionate people who design some of the world's most eye-catching baby and toddler strollers, prams, etc. I visited the Cosatto headquarters in Bolton and, similar to the Moneypenny experience, I mirrored the faces of the entire team that day with a big smile of my own.

From the simple yet imaginative telephone entry system, to the must go on, most talked about office show stopper. Yes, of course you can take the stairs or lift, but who wouldn't want to slide down from the office to the showroom?

The final piece of building the internal foundations was the Cosatto awards ceremony. Stood at the back of the room, I observed multiple awards given out to the team. Everyone in the organisation was able to vote. And there were literally hundreds of gifts and prizes to choose from. There was also a special once-in-a-lifetime award where the staff would choose the one thing they'd love to do. It was wonderful to witness the buzz and camaraderie within the room that day where the atmosphere was palpable.

Moving slightly away from the business world to a sports club that delivered a unique form of Celebrity Service to every fan past, present and future. Reading Football Club registered their fans as an official member of the squad.

Since 2001 no player can wear the number 13 jersey as this belongs to their loyal and royal supporters. What did this cost the club?

What gestures could you make to your clients, customers, members or fans to make them feel special and a part of what you do?

NUMBER 13

Reading Football Club became the first club to register its fans as an official member of the squad, allocating squad number 13 to 'Reading Fans' in August 2001.

CELEBRITY

Late Middle English (in the sense "solemn ceremony"): from Old French celebrite or Latin celebritas, from celebrar, celebr- "frequented or honoured".

To help you explore the concept of Celebrity Service in more detail, I've broken it down into bite-sized chunks:

Consistency
Excitement
Love
Engagement
Bravado
Response
Independence
Thank You
You and Your Team

Each area looks at the standout brands and people who deliver "Celebrity Service". Whether or not you are a celebrity would make very little difference in what they said, what they did, or how they reacted.

If you think of the wondrous sights and sounds of South Africa, you probably think of Table Top mountain, Kruger Park, or maybe Spion Kop. For me, I make a beeline for one place, and one place only: my favourite petrol station in the world.

I first wrote about Alison and her chalkboard sign outside her BP garage in the OMG book, and revelled in how creative and cost-effective this one idea had become. It's one of my all-time favourite stories, and can also be viewed on my YouTube channel. You see, for over 40 years, Alison and her family have written a message, joke, quote, or quip on the board, to put a smile on motorists' faces along Jan Smuts Avenue in Johannesburg.

This is not only genius marketing, but what I am about to reveal is the reason why I have included her (again) here... No matter what happens in your business, consistency is the key to service delivery.

In December 2013, one Facebook post left a lump in my throat.

It was the day Nelson Mandela died and for the first time Alison put down her chalk and hung a black veil over the sign as a mark of respect. During the mourning period, every message she wrote was a quote from the great man and former President.

It was a wonderfully touching thing to do, and a small yet clever mark of respect.

Months later I returned to South Africa (avoiding the tourist sights and sounds) and headed out to see Alison and the board again.

To my dismay, everything was closed. The forecourt was dug up, diggers were strewn everywhere, and a high metal fence perimeter was erected. The business was shut.

But not the sign.

Here is what I snapped:

Is there anything worse than inconsistency in customer service? Where you never know what to expect from day to day? This one example proves that no matter what state your business may be in, you should never give up in consistently pleasing the customer.

**FOOTBALL IS 90 MINS OF PRETENDING YOU'RE HURT
RUGBY IS 80 MINS OF PRETENDING YOU'RE NOT!!!!!**

How do you become number one on TripAdvisor?

How do you consistently stay at number one, for years?

Is it the cleanliness of the rooms? Is it the warm welcome from the team? Is it the email directions before you leave? Is it the amazing amount of "things to do" including a book that you wrote and published just for the guests? Could it be the numerous trails you created for the children, or the pool, the games room, or many of the outdoor activities? Just what is it? Well, in the heart of Cornwall I think I may have found the answer and it's not what you'd think or possibly believe.

When you consistently put parents before profits, providing them with a true escape from the hamster wheel of home life, then maybe, just maybe you can establish your business as the number one in your sector.

Let me introduce you to Nanny Pat and Farmer Dave. They own Bosinver Farm Cottages near St Austell, Cornwall. Now, I must confess I've known Pat for a long time (she first came to see me present in Redruth over a decade ago) and we have stayed friends ever since. This year Pat and Dave invited us down for a week's holiday with Grace and Elliot and, despite all of the great things I've mentioned already, it was the sense of giving, supporting and helping parents that astounded both Hayley and I.

Let me take you on a guided tour to show you what I mean...

In the games room there were numerous activities including jenga, table tennis, a pool table and an arcade machine (and everything was on free vend)! No need for parents to scrap around for change and spend an unnecessary fortune during their stay. Oh, and if you fancy watching a blockbuster that evening you can choose from hundreds of DVDs (all free). You'll find the DVDs in the laundry room which incidentally has all the soap and conditioner you'll need (all for free).

Oh, it's starting to rain and we haven't brought our raincoats. No problem, simply choose your favourite colour and style and it's yours (free of charge). Oh, look the sun's come out again, let's have a barbeque (don't buy a disposable one – Nanny Pat and Farmer Dave have supplied it all for you free of charge). It's raining again (help yourself to wellies). Fancy a trip to the beach? (Windbreakers, bodyboards, they are all yours free of charge.) Feeling sporty? You can see where we are going with this.

And then there are some nights when you really can't be bothered to cook. So, you can simply pop into the reception area, open up the fridge freezer and there you'll find a range of homemade meals from Angels in the Kitchen (there is a charge to be made in the honesty box, but Bosinver don't put any mark-up on the meals at all). It's the same with the beauty and massage treatments. Local beauticians use the room free of charge as Pat and Dave want to give local businesses a helping hand.

NB: On arriving, the greatest cream sponge cake will be awaiting you in the fridge. It is with regret that I did not manage to get to my camera before Grace and Elliot got to the cake.

70% of guests re-book. And I now know why. When you consistently put service before profit, helping, supporting and providing for your customers, the good reviews and re-bookings will forever flood in.

How can your business demonstrate...

CONSISTENCY?

CELEBRITY
SERVICE

Can you name a member of cabin crew from any of the flights you've ever taken? Possibly, but more probably not. Over the years, an incredible amount of publicity has justifiably been given to the wonderful service on-board South West Airlines in the United States, and by now, like me, you've probably watched many viral videos they have featured in. There was no video camera to capture this trip, but the person I am about to share with you is quite simply the greatest cabin crew member of all time.

She brought excitement to the passengers in just 90 minutes. I'd just finished speaking at a conference in Harare, Zimbabwe. Having arrived at the airport, I quickly received my boarding card.

Glancing at it, I was mildly excited to see I was sat in 1F. I'd been upgraded! (I was wearing my three-piece suit after all.)

Now, I have a lot more confidence in larger planes than I do smaller ones. We were called to our gate and walked onto the tarmac. But there was no plane to be seen, only a tiny aircraft with propellers in the distance. Yes, this was our plane. On the horizon, huge black clouds started to engulf the city and the sounds of rumbling thunder and the odd fork lightning flash lit up the skies. I was becoming nervous thinking by the time we board the plane the storm would be upon us. I walked up the stairs and was met by two cabin crew.

"Good afternoon, sir. Can we see your boarding card?"

"Yes, certainly." (But I could not find which pocket in my suit I'd put it in.)

"Oh, we do apologise, sir…"

"No, that's okay. Here it is."

She paused, looking at my upgraded ticket, and then she lent in and whispered, "Oh… you have won a prize!"

"What have I won?"

"I can't tell you now, but I will soon."

I walked a few short steps and took my seat beside an older gentleman (the propelled plane was so small we were in Economy!). I turned to the gentleman and said, "Did you win a prize?"

"Yes, but she wouldn't tell me what it was."

At this point, the people in the row across the aisle turned to us and said that they had also been told they were prizewinners.

Being sat at the front gave me a great vantage point as I could hear every single conservation as the rest of the passengers boarded. What struck me was that everyone received a compliment, and I mean everyone. Whether it was about their clothes, hair or even about the toys being carried by children as they boarded with their parents.

Everyone was buckled in and we started to taxi. The cabin crew member then picked up the phone and announced to everyone that she was delighted everyone was on board and then proceeded to say, "And you have the best-looking cabin crew serving you today," with a sarcastic smile.

She asked very politely if everyone would take out of their front pockets the safety instructions and read them, as it would really help us all should an incident occur.

I looked around and for the first time ever – everyone did! The phone was put down and she leant into the first row, aka the prizewinners, and said, "Here's your prize: you have just won the chance to help me open the door should there be an emergency." Well, we all fell about laughing.

We'd been in the air for 30 minutes and the drinks trolley came through. As First Class/ Economy front-row passengers, we were first up. She served the gentleman to my left:

"Would you like a drink, sir?"

"Yes, please, a water."

"Would you like ice with that?"

"No, thanks."

"Oh, you're way too cool for ice..." Again, we raised our eyebrows and laughed at this engaging, yet exciting, service.

Halfway back to South Africa, I took the short walk to the front of the plane and spoke to her and told her that what she had done from take off to now had been brilliant and that she indeed gives great Celebrity Service. Ladies and gentlemen, meet Christina (left). She works on AirLink, a part of South African Airways. Celebrity Service – the ability to provide customer service to everyone, not just celebrities.

I booked Hayley and her best friend Sharon into Frasers Suites Edinburgh. They are huge Robbie Williams fans and the concert was being held at the iconic Murrayfield Stadium in Scotland.

When I made the booking I mentioned why they were travelling north of the border. Frasers logged this "tiny" piece of detail and began to create an incredible piece of Celebrity Service.

As Hayley and Sharon entered their room, this is what the team had composed on a note. For any Robbie fans, read closely. For the non-Robbie fans, you may have guessed by now that the words "Angels", "Kids" and "Strong" are all of his hit songs. How amazing is this? Celebrity Service lies in amongst the finest of details.

And the final comment I'll make in this article is one of pride. You see Frasers are one of my clients.

Thank you, Frasers. Can't wait to spend more "Lazy Days" in your fabulous properties.

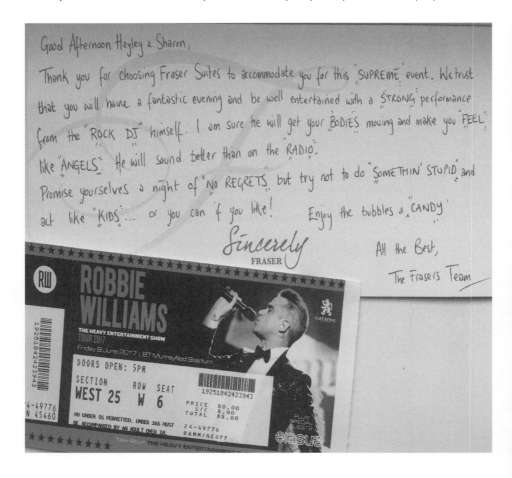

Now there's a name I've not heard in a long time.

Did you know that if a guest, client or associate were to visit your offices you have three choices in which to welcome them? Each one says an awful lot about you and the customer experience culture within your organisation. So what do these three options look like?

1. You do nothing – they aren't really that important to you after all, and, hey, they'll find a parking space somewhere I am sure. This sadly accounts for 99% of businesses you'll attend this week. (I made this figure up but it could be higher.)

2. You personalise the welcome. Ah, yes, for that client you hope to win over. You have had this visit in your diary for some time; you know you are one of three companies pitching for the work. So maybe, just maybe, you'll add their name to the sandwich board or sign. Great thinking, but still quite a rarity.

3. But what about the third option? This one belongs in the "celebrity" category and is only available to Brad, George, Angelina, Tom (Hardy, Cruise take your pick), and Cameron (Diaz not David). But will you have time to do it? Will you or your team even consider this as an option to begin with? Yes, you personalise the welcome, but then you make it one of a kind, something that will bring about the biggest of smiles (or laughter) at the sight of it for that guest, client or associate.

The image you are seeing is, of course, option 3. It was brilliantly created by the wonderful team at Profound Services based in Peterlee, County Durham. I have known the Managing Director, Steven Ward, since the day he started his business back in 2006. As so often happens after an internal session for the team, many of the delegates connect with me on LinkedIn, Twitter and Facebook and if anyone glances for just a second, they'll see I have a love for a well-known movie franchise.

When I visited their offices recently they made the jump to hyper space and landed right into option 3. This is a company that puts the clients at the heart of everything they do and I am immensely proud to know and work with them all.

So the question is this, which of the three will you deliver tomorrow? Post your ideas and images to me at geoff@geofframm.com and I'll look forward to showcasing you one day.

How can your business create...

EXCITEMENT?

CELEBRITY
SERVICE

It would have been rather an easy "L" to have chosen Loyalty within the Celebrity breakdown.

Loyalty, of course, is brought on by great service wrapped around a great product or brand. The next step would then be advocacy, personified for me by the Apple brand. Meet an iPhone, iPad or mac user and you'll come across an advocate born out of loyalty for the product and its support.

Where else in the world would you receive high fives from the staff as they open their doors to a new store or launch a new product?

'L' in celebrity is quite simply Love. As Lennon & McCartney wrote:

"There's nothing you can do that can't be done.

"Nothing you can do but you can learn how to be you in time – It's easy."

You simply have to love delivering fantastic service. Not just in the great times of "nothing is wrong", but also when the blame is on you, when you have made a mistake, and when things just aren't going according to plan.

The weekend was planned months in advance; a chance to celebrate a friend's birthday, free from the husbands, enjoying some pampering beauty treatments, and the chance to lie in without little ones bouncing on the bed at 5am.

However, on the train on the way to the capital three of the four ladies received a call on their mobiles explaining that their previously booked spa treatments would need to be rearranged due to a member of staff ringing in sick that day. The ladies were all naturally disappointed, as the weekend had been planned to the minute, however, the hotel said they would sort something out upon their arrival. As promised, upon arrival the group were met with a huge apology and given the time to go through the system to make sure another suitable time slot could be arranged.

Two of the three booked for treatments were able to go ahead with another time, so not an ideal situation but it had been well handled and, therefore, the group were able to just move on to the next part of their planned weekend.

The story doesn't end there, however, as when the ladies went to their rooms later that day to drop in their luggage they were met with a personalised note and a goodie bag of gifts as an apology for any disruption – a display of sheer love of service.

When it goes wrong, we put it right, not just with an apology but with an offer, but not just with an offer, but with a further discount, and a goodie bag (whatever that may be), and a letter, card or note that is personalised. Natalie at the Apex in Edinburgh gets it. She has independence to make these decisions and does the right thing.

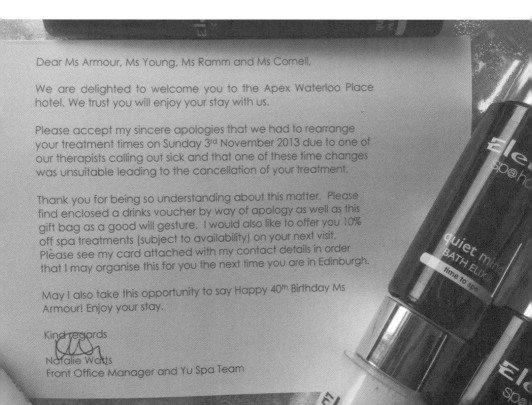

Dear Ms Armour, Ms Young, Ms Ramm and Ms Cornell,

We are delighted to welcome you to the Apex Waterloo Place hotel. We trust you will enjoy your stay with us.

Please accept my sincere apologies that we had to rearrange your treatment times on Sunday 3rd November 2013 due to one of our therapists calling out sick and that one of these time changes was unsuitable leading to the cancellation of your treatment.

Thank you for being so understanding about this matter. Please find enclosed a drinks voucher by way of apology as well as this gift bag as a good will gesture. I would also like to offer you 10% off spa treatments (subject to availability) on your next visit. Please see my card attached with my contact details in order that I may organise this for you the next time you are in Edinburgh.

May I also take this opportunity to say Happy 40th Birthday Ms Armour! Enjoy your stay.

Kind regards

Natalie Watts
Front Office Manager and Yu Spa Team

When things breakdown there are three ways to communicate this to your customers or clients. They are as follows:

First option: A hotel in the heart of Manchester put this notice on their games machine in the foyer. Straight to the point. No messing around here. Out of order. Sorry.

Second option: The outdoor holiday camp, Center Parcs. When the drinks machine was out of order they apologised and said their team are working on it. No, I don't know how long it will take to be fixed but it's a step in the right direction.

And then there's option number three: Apologise, yes, show the personality behind your brand and communicate with love. The best examples I've seen of this are from the INTU Shopping Malls. Here are two of my favourites...

SUZUKI SPEED

It took just 24 hours to turn a mundane sign into something customers could read with a smile. The Luscombe Suzuki showroom in Leeds was transformed into a mini conference area for the whole team for a Celebrity Service interactive session. Before I started, I popped into the toilet and on the door was the following sign:

IF YOU ARE UNHAPPY IN ANY WAY WITH THE CONDITION OF THE TOILETS PLEASE CONTACT PETE BRANDON ON THE SUZUKI SERVICE DESK

There's nothing really wrong with this message, although I did think being in UPPER CASE it could be construed as a little AGGRESSIVE. I quickly took the photograph and inserted it into the talk that evening. I then challenged the team to create a greater more friendly notice to customers. Twenty-four hours later Managing Director, Robin Luscombe, and Marketing Comms manager, Jane Whyman, had great pleasure in sending me the image of the new Suzuki toilet sign the team had created.

What pieces of communication are in and around your business right now, and what can you do to improve them? Please send me your before and after shots.

CUSTOMER IS KING - OR QUEEN
AT LUSCOMBE'S
If you consider this throne is not fit for royalty, please do let one of the courtiers (members of staff) know

I tip my hat off to every event planner who organises conferences, as they need to literally tick a hundred boxes to ensure its success. Choosing the right venue, audio visual team, accommodation, menus, timings, speakers, themes, awards, transportation and dinners, the list is almost endless. If your event is all about the attendees then here are two organisations that could really inspire you.

Every year the financial planning specialists, Centrepoint, based in Brisbane, choose some of the most iconic countries and settings to host their global event. However, Mel Lamb and the team always choose to go one step further, by making the very first touchpoints extra special for the attendees who have travelled all the way from Australia. This was my welcome plaque at Cape Town airport:

NB: Sand dancer is someone born in South Shields (the devil is in the detail).

And once in the room delegates received a wonderful handmade gift by Clothed In Hope, which is an organisation empowering women in Zambia. Notice the gifts were for my family – Hayley, Grace and Elliot.

Before the Best Western Conference in Brighton, Nicola Adie, Senior Events Manager, contacted all of the delegates and asked for their "Stand Out" story from each hotel. After collating the information, they then set about transforming the corridors of the venue into a celebration of the delegates' success. Imagine seeing your name strewn everywhere for everyone to see? So they printed the achievements onto golden stars and stuck them on the tiled floors similar to what you'd see along the Hollywood Boulevard itself.

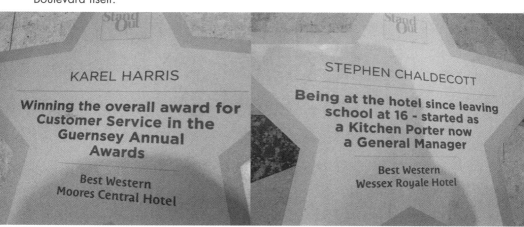

KAREL HARRIS

Winning the overall award for Customer Service in the Guernsey Annual Awards

Best Western
Moores Central Hotel

STEPHEN CHALDECOTT

Being at the hotel since leaving school at 16 - started as a Kitchen Porter now a General Manager

Best Western
Wessex Royale Hotel

How can your business show...

LOVE?

CELEBRITY

SERVICE

Engagement has been one of the buzziest of buzz words in marketing and service for some time now (and rightly so), but what I want to challenge you with is not only engaging the customer who holds the purse strings, but to seek out opportunities to engage their nearest and dearest too.

Our favourite family theme park in the world has to be Portaventura in Spain. The attractions are for all ages, the weather is always great, but it's the little things for the little ones that make this place so special.

Customer Service starts well before you even get into the room. The concierge welcomed us to the hotel and parked our car whilst we took Grace inside to the special themed room check-in desk.

We sat down and before we could say who we were and how many nights we'd be staying, the lady behind the desk said to Grace, "Oh, I have something for you... Woody asked me specifically to give this to you when you got here." Grace's face was beaming at this point as the lady reached down, opened the drawer of her desk, and pulled out a plush Woody Woodpecker soft toy.

We then started to check-in, and throughout this process between the grown-ups, the lady frequently paused to speak to Grace or to ask her a question.

"That's it," she said. "Woody has just told me your room is ready, and later on you can see him in the park, and, of course, tomorrow morning for breakfast. C'mon lets go..." As she got up she held out her hand to Grace and the pair of them walked together out of the lobby with us following behind. We went up in the tree lift (a lift painted to look like a tree) and were led to our room – Grace was shown in first, of course. Once we were in there were more gifts, including a bathroom set which she still has to this day.

Take a trip to Birmingham International train station in the UK and, if you look down, you'll come across this wonderful service engagement for canine travellers. Whether you are travelling first class, standard, on or off peak, Virgin Trains provide fresh water for their canine customers before they board the train.

On the subject of our four-legged friends, a good friend from my college days sadly had to say goodbye to her 15-year-old West Highland White Terrier. She said her final goodbye and a few days later received a sympathy card from the veterinary surgery… the card and the pre-printed words were probably enough, but what tipped it into the celebrity category was the power of the written word, and the time and effort taken to comfort the customer.

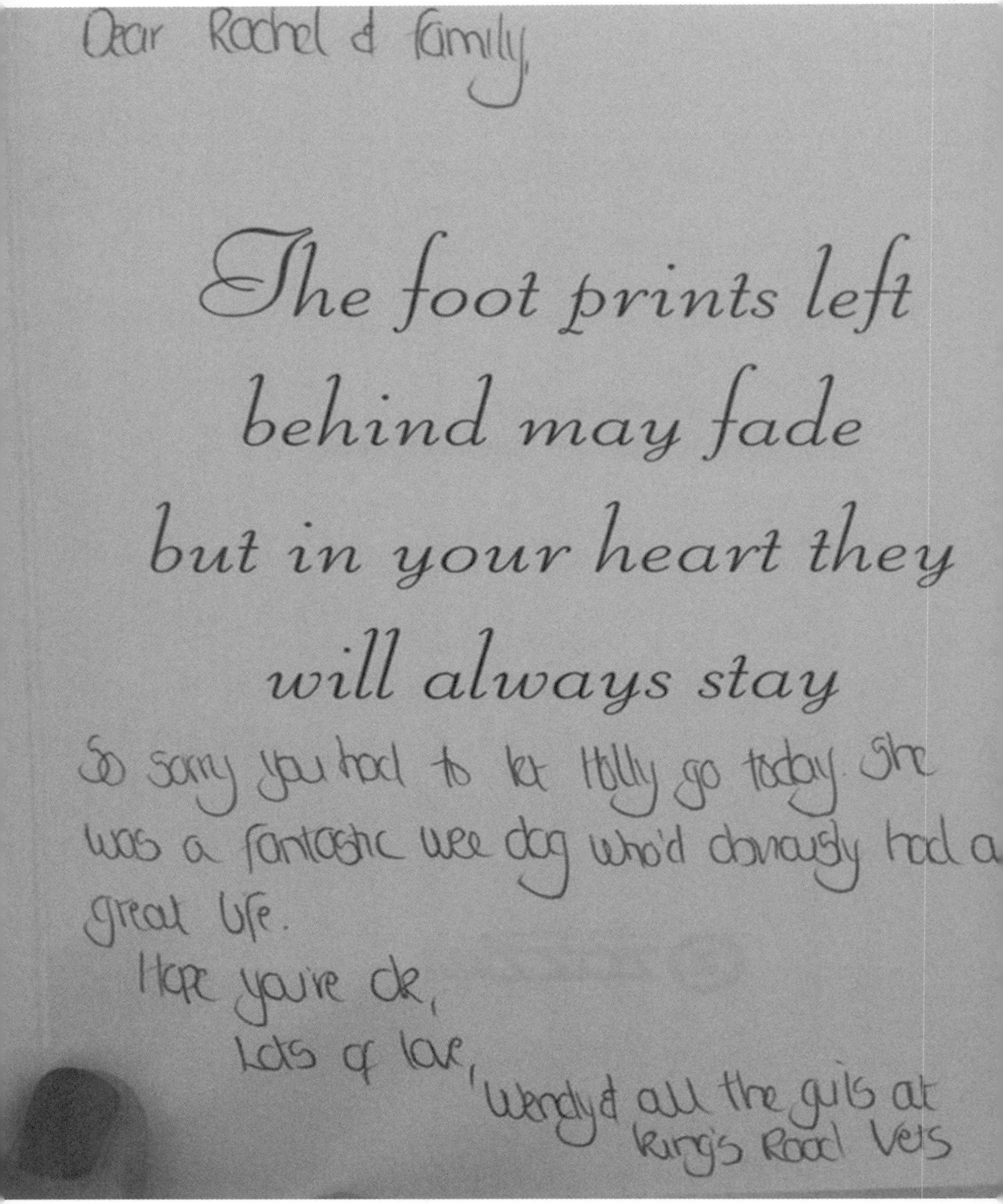

Dear Rachel & family,

The foot prints left behind may fade but in your heart they will always stay

So sorry you had to let Holly go today. She was a fantastic wee dog who'd obviously had a great life.

Hope you're ok,

Lots of love,

Wendy & all the girls at King's Road Vets

Hats off to Premier Inn, Derby West, for engaging / hooking the attention of Grace and her friend once they entered their family hotel room.

Sitting on the bed were two little plastic yellow ducks on top of a note, which read...

Moments later they were running down the hotel hallway (faces beaming) and into the reception area. They were met by one of the most welcoming reception staff I've ever seen, who became as giddy as the children as she reached for the "tasty treats".

Great creative ideas like this don't cost the earth, but they engage our nearest and dearest, which sets the tone for a great experience with that brand.

Now what could you do?

Elliot wanted to go on a BIG train. So we arrived at Newcastle Central Station to take a one-hour trip to either York or Berwick upon Tweed. As we entered the Virgin East Coast ticket office I walked up to the lady behind the counter, Pam Thompson, to ask when the next available train would be.

She said, "There's an Edinburgh-bound train arriving in 11 minutes."

"Great. Can I have two tickets, please?"

"How old is your son?" she asked.

"Four," I said.

"Under fives are free, so he doesn't need a ticket." Now, how many of you reading this would stop there? You've given the customer some good news, but could you go even further?

She continued, "But I am pretty sure he'd really like one. What's his name?"

"Elliot," I replied.

She took a blank card out of the machine, picked up a pen and wrote three words. She handed the ticket to me and I passed it to Elliot whose face lit up.

You have no idea how much he loved this gesture. Three simple ways to bring excitement into your customer touchpoints: 1. Give what you don't need to; 2. Personalise where you can; 3. Add a touch of magic.

This was the image I posted on Facebook, later that day I also shot a celebrity video for my YouTube channel. (Take a look and you'll see Elliot making a cameo appearance.) I also tweeted the video to Virgin Trains, who in turn re-tweeted it to over 138,000 followers.

What will you do today to create a buzz around your business for the experience you gave?

I'd been told by so many people, "Ooh, you'll love the Disney experience" and "the service you'll get from day one will be world class." So I couldn't wait to sample it all for myself. Of course, we all know Mickey Mouse, but does he really know you?

To enter the parks you have a guest pass card. When it's your turn to enter through the barrier you simultaneously scan the pass card whilst placing your index finger on the machine. Once it glows green the staff member on the other side greets you as you walk through. But it's the greeting that is right up there in the world of Celebrity Service.

Grace and Elliot were first up, excited at scanning their own pass. When they walked through they were met with, "Good morning, Elliot" or "Hello, Grace, Welcome to Disney". Within moments the children turned around with a huge beam on their face..."Ooh, how do they know us?" Of course, on the other side of the machine the names of the people are displayed for the staff to view and then the staff use this information to deliver a personalised welcome.

Soon after the initial personalised welcome you can actually pick up a free badge (a large pin badge – not a sticker that lasts 10 mins). There were only three to choose from and not everyone could receive one. So, if it's your very first time at Disney, you got a badge or if it was your birthday that day or you were celebrating your anniversary, you also received a badge.

So the Ramm family proudly donned their pin badges. But what do you think happens for the duration of your badge-wearing day? What I observed was something rather special, obvious, but special and something I can't believe any other theme parks have not yet adopted. Throughout the day and night, staff members would notice your coloured badge from across the street and yell out, "Happy birthday", "Happy anniversary" or "Welcome to your first time at Disney". With all of the attractions and shows taking place during your stay you can easily forget you have the badge on, but the team certainly don't let you forget it's your special day.

When the parks open there is a huge surge towards the rides and attractions from the people who could not obtain fast pass tickets. As the queues start to swell and the baristas tap their coffee beans to serve the early risers, I observed the only areas of the parks that were empty at this stage were the stores full of merchandise.

So what do the staff do when no one is coming to visit them? Stock the shelves? Get a caffeine fix of their own? No. They simply come out onto the pavement wearing a large Mickey Mouse glove and stand waving and welcoming everyone as you walk past.

All of these three techniques showed willing, didn't really cost much to do and made a big impact on the guests.

The last time I had my eyes checked I must have been chewing Hubba Bubba and swapping Panini football stickers. Decades on, I walked through the doors of the SpecSavers opticians store in Washington, Tyne & Wear. However, I was there as a double agent. Firstly to have a long overdue eye test, but also to observe the customer service and experience from every touchpoint. A few months later I would be speaking to over a thousand SpecSavers managers at their annual conference, so I was undercover.

The service, attention to detail and friendliness of the staff were second to none, and I received the 20/20 thumbs up for my vision. All good, but everything can be improved upon. Right?

Although the front of house team receive many plaudits and customer service accolades, the laboratory technicians who create the glasses out back, had very little interaction with the customer. In the run up to the event, the team shared with me an opportunity they had spotted by way of a small piece of card, which could be used by the technicians to write their name on so the customer knew who had made the glasses. A very nice touchpoint.

However, in the build up to the conference I spotted an opportunity for the number one optical brand in the UK to create additional engagement. After the main stage keynote I then delivered a Celebrity Service interactive session for the highly-skilled technicians. And I opened up with the following:

"So, you have a card to write your name on. And the only thing you know about the customer you've never met is their name, and the type of glasses they are buying. So let's turn this card into an amazing piece of engagement."

And then started the very first 120 Minute Challenge.

"If you knew the next pair of frames were the Star Wars or Disney Princess design, and you knew the girl's or boy's names – what could you possibly write on your new card?"

Cue a creative buzz in the room as everyone gathered on their tables to work as a team to come up with ideas. I counted down the final five seconds and stopped the clock. Everyone put down their pens. With a roving mic I walked around each table and asked the teams to share their ideas. The answers that came back from the lab technicians that day were some of the very best I'd heard. From "These are the glasses you've been looking for" to "Elsa thinks you look beautiful in these", the idea had stuck.

Celebrity Service is all about spotting the opportunities and then taking them. Of course, not every branch has their own technicians out back, and not every pair can lend themselves to something so personalised, but after giving your teams license to unleash their creativity, wonderful engaging moments can occur.

Jack Ismail, Partnership Director at SpecSavers said, "We are always looking to differentiate our offer and to stand out from the rest of the high street. We have an incredible suite of high-tech optical and audiology equipment to ensure our customers have the best experience. The most memorable customer experiences, however, have more to do with the fantastic colleagues in our stores who really have the power to make a difference for customers. The Celebrity Service message has really gotten our people thinking about how they personalise and create memorable experiences for our customers... and Geoff has inspired our teams to think about this. As one Partner remarked to me yesterday... 'I could listen to Geoff's stories about celebrity service all day long!'"

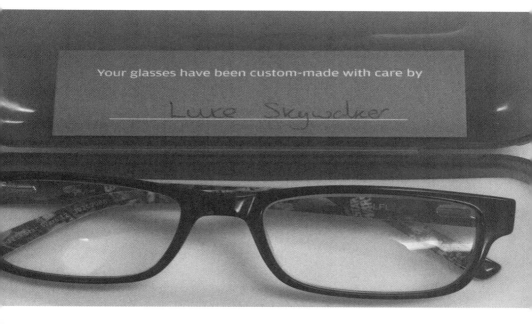

How can you bring

ENGAGEMENT

to your customers?

CELEBRITY

SERVICE

Picture the scene: 11:30pm on a cold night in Edinburgh, Scotland. I was on my way to see the Edinburgh Fringe Festival from my hotel near the Haymarket. On the way back I passed a bike shop (push bikes rather than motorised) called, The Bike Smith. By now the shop must have been closed for five or six hours; the shutters were down, there was no contact number, no help sheets outside, and no one around, and yet they were still providing service! But how?

Take a closer look at the image on the next page… they simply chained up a large foot pump and left it outside for any cyclist who needed extra air in their tyres!

Would you risk having something stolen to ensure you were serving your customers out of hours? This was not only brave, but a genius service idea.

A PERSIAN PROMISE...

Back in November 2009, I embarked on my very first trip to Iran to speak at the World Advertising & Branding Forum. Our plane landed into Tehran airport at 1:00am, and was followed by a further one-hour drive to the hotel. As soon as I was in the car, I switched on my phone to text home to say I'd arrived safely. There was nothing! No signal, no nothing! But that's okay, I'll phone when I get to the hotel room.

2:30am, I tried calling home, but after many attempts at dialling a variety of numbers, it would still not connect.

3:00am, decision made to open up the laptop, connect to the internet and email / send messages via social media. You know where this is heading now... Countless attempts, and no successful connection.

Now worry had turned into mild panic: this call was important and needed to be made.

3:15am I got into the lift and headed to the reception desk. I spoke to the concierge and explained my situation. "Ahh, no problem, Mr Geoff, I shall connect you through our telephone..." Yep, you guessed it, we could not connect.

3:45pm Mild Panic had progressed to Moderate Hysteria.

"Please, Mr Geoff, I will look after this for you. I promise! Please give me your wife's email address and I shall email her for you."

"Are you sure?"

"Yes, I promise. And if she emails you back I will print it out and let you see it straight away."

4:00am, the sun is rising and I get my head down for two hours' sleep. Now, imagine your partner is away for the very first time on the other side of the world, and they had promised to let you know they had arrived and, more importantly, that they were safe. Then you received the following email:

Dear Mrs Geoff,
We have your husband. Do not worry he is safe.

A promise is a promise, and Hotel Persian Evin certainly delivered, perhaps not in the carefully crafted words we would have liked to ensure comfort and security, but they did what they said they were going to do.

Luckily, I was able to get in touch with Hayley the next day to reassure her that I really was ok!

For decades the ice-cream experience has been the same old, same old. Your options (if you can call them that) are: a cone with a scoop or a tub with multiple scoops. And then came the chocolate flake, the raspberry sauce, the sprinkles and, of course, the hot chocolate or fudge sauce.

That's it.

But what if there were a third option? You know the one that looks so amazing every customer wants it. And they are prepared to spend so much more money to have it.

So you launch your own ice-cream parlour and on the very first day the customer comes to you and says "Ice cream please"... "Certainly, what would you like?" The customer peruses the options and then gets to the third one. "OMG do you do that?" "Yes," you reply. Without hesitation they order the third one. NB: This option is more than twice the price of the other two!

The challenge is what does your third option look like? You can create absolutely anything you wish. Money is no barrier. Be as creative, crazy and outlandish as you need to be – just make it the greatest experience the customer has ever known.

Your two minutes has just started...

N-ICE Experience: _____

_____

_____

_____

_____

What I am about to show you was the ice cream I ordered at the Dubai Mall. Turn to page 131 to see the n-ice, third option, experience come to life.

SNAP DECISION

So I am at the Park Inn hotel in Krakov, Poland, for the Kodak Conference. I've set up my mac and props by the stage and completed a sound check in the main conference room. As I approach the table, I notice three stations of tea, coffee, pastries, fruit and chilled drinks. As I approach I notice the conference branding is in full swing. There are meters of Kodak film paper around the cups and saucers, film reels and clapper boards made out of icing on top of the cupcakes and a large movie camera placed on top of a crate. Brilliant ideas to ensure the brand flows throughout the entire event.

I return to the room and speak to Johanna from Kodak and compliment her on the decoration outside. Her reply leaves me speechless.

"Oh, we didn't do that, it was the hotel."

So the team at the Park Inn knew who was coming months in advance, no doubt had a meeting to see how they could create a greater experience for the client, and this was the result. Bravo.

How can you show

BRAVADO

in your business?

CELEBRITY
SERVICE

Whenever I think of the word "Response" in customer service I can't help thinking about the "You must pick up the phone within three rings!" scenario.

However, forget two rings, three rings or a whopping Olympic sized five rings. This form of response concentrates on the art of how you can respond: not with time, but with technology, and how you can stand out from the crowd by personalising whilst surprising your customers.

There's a BMW Mini garage just a mile from our home which we pass most days in the car. Outside of the showroom for everyone to see there is a bright pink (think Lady Penelope from Thunderbirds colour) Mini Cooper. Of course, no one would buy it. It would surely depreciate very quickly, but it certainly turns heads… one head in particular was Grace's. Grace loves the car and had been asking to go to see it for some time.

As luck or bad luck would have it, Hayley's car had just broken down and she was in the market for a new car. Days later, Hayley and Grace went to the showroom, saw a car they liked, and Grace got to take a closer look at her little pink dream. Details were exchanged and the saleswoman from BMW Mini said she would send out further information.

Hayley came home expecting the usual car-sales collateral to be sent out, maybe a folder with inserts and prices of the car, a DVD, or an email with pictures and further details.

None of the above materialised; what she promptly received was a video email which the saleswoman had recorded on her phone or camera, going into greater detail as she filmed around the car.

Now at this point I need to stress the quality was not great, it was taken 90 degrees on its side, the sales pitch could have been so much better, but this did not matter – this was different, this was personal, and this made Hayley feel special.

Response is not just the time you take to respond, but with the exciting technology at our disposal we can respond in a different, and in a highly personalised way. However, the real element of "Celebrity Service" was still to come. A second email pinged onto the laptop, from the same woman, featuring a second video made just for Grace, featuring the bright pink Mini.

Celebrity Response is not just how fast you come back to the customer, but how creative you are in doing so. How could you respond using similar technology?

Having a better response, whether it be a personalised video or giving help in store to frequent customer requests gives you an undoubted competitive edge. But if you can add a little humour into proceedings you can diffuse a situation very quickly. Now, you may well be taking a risk at this point as not everyone frequents a comedy store each week and is willing to play with you. However, delivered and played well it can give any dissatisfied customer reason to think you are brilliant. For example, me.

Geoff Ramm @GeoffRamm · 4 Nov 2015
C'mon @flybe your website crashes more than a tie fighter!

11:35 AM - 4 Nov 2015 · Details

Flybe ✈ ✓
@flybe

Following

@GeoffRamm Hi Geoff, I'm sorry that you have had problems with the website again. The web... goo.gl/562Mk2

Geoff Ramm @GeoffRamm · 4 Nov 2015
@flybe hahaha love the pic! I am trying to book Newcastle to Ston 18th Dec - is there a number to best call Faye?

View other replies

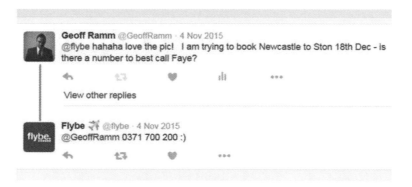

Flybe ✈ @flybe · 4 Nov 2015
@GeoffRamm 0371 700 200 :)

LOST LUGGAGE, LOST BUSINESS

With the aim of shopping for a good carry-on case for short haul flights, I walked into a store not far from me in a retail outlet village. Having picked up a couple of cases, I asked the two staff members which size was allowable on planes.

"We don't know," was the abrupt reply by one, whilst the other said, "Every plane is different so you'll never know which to take unless you know the carrier you are flying with."

And with that, I left the store.

There was another luggage shop in the retail village. I walked in, found the case I liked, and asked the same question.

"Ah," said the lady, "let me show you this…" She took me to the front of the store, removed a large case from the shelf, and there behind it was a size chart for different carriers, detailing what they would and would not accept as hand luggage.

A different service, aided by knowledge and aided by the fact they had answers ready for this type of question.

What questions are you regularly asked? What questions could you be asked? Do you have the answers ready for anyone who comes to you?

I bought two cases from that store, a smaller, hand-held one and a larger case for a few nights away. They were on a buy-one-get-one-free offer. I've recommended the shop ever since.

It's easy to sell when you help.

In the land of Father Christmas you'll wait all year round for him to visit you, and when he does, it tends to be an unforgettable experience. But what would happen if you reversed it? And you chose to visit Finland for yourself.

My own personal experiences of visiting this wonderful country will stay with me forever and it is all down to one particular brand and the Nordic experience they give.

Finnair are the national carrier and one of the leading fleets in the skies. Here are the trio of celebrity-thinking ideas I experienced:

1. When talking to some of their crew they told me about two very special gifts they gave passengers. One was a book based on the *Tales Of A Thousand And One Flights* and the other was a children's book called *Airy Tales*. They were placed on the seats as a gift for both adults and passengers as they boarded. But there was a twist. The books were entirely written and illustrated by the cabin crew, pilots and ground staff at Finnair.

2. The second example is something I shall never forget and, sadly, I can't show you it here. However, if you type Geoff Ramm Finnair into YouTube, you'll see for yourself. To inform the crews that I was coming to Helsinki, Suvi Saarela and Mira Hamalainen-Iho created a welcome video in what can only be described as a Hollywood trailer in the making!

3. When I arrived the team had made up a special welcome basket of goodies, but best of all was the traditional Finnish Munovi recipe which Suvi had prepared herself.

A question to ask yourself and your business: "What can our team create, handmake or deliver?"

I'd quite happily issue a challenge to any airline that has created such a welcome to its passengers and guests.

Airborne

TALES FROM A THOUSAND AND ONE FLIGHTS

FINNAIR

RIITTA KIIVERI • TONY POKKINEN
NOORA KUNTTU • PIRKKO SAARI • CHRISTINA STRANDBERG
MERIITTA ANTIKARI • KATI KAIVANTO • LENE MALMSTRÖM

AIRY TALES

Stories fro
above
the clouds
and beyond the Sk

Editors Tirpa Kivilaakso, Riitta Kiiveri ja
Anna-Brotta Pietilä

What kind of
RESPONSE
should you provide?

CELEBRITY
SERVICE

For some, Customer Service is written up in a rule book for staff to follow.

But in the world of "Celebrity Service" there are no rules; it's a blank canvas, where the answer invariably starts with, "Yes".

Being a fan of American Football, I went for a tour of the Lincoln Financial stadium, home of the Philadelphia Eagles. Having stood pitch-side, sat in an executive box on the 50-yard line, and checked out the locker rooms, I proceeded to the store and, as well as a jersey, soft toy eagle and a shiny Eagles helmet, I bought a sun visor hat for Hayley. Back at the hotel, whilst looking through my purchases, I noticed the electronic tag was still attached (I have no idea how I got through the security doors).

Not having time to go back to the stadium, I entered a clothes store in downtown Philly but they could not remove it as they don't stock it. The second store was the same. At this point and on my third attempt I felt like the big bad wolf and, cap in hand, I entered Macy's department store. Within moments the shop assistant had removed the tag and even put the visor in one of their bags! Like the others, she did not have to as they did not stock this item. But you have to ask yourself the golden question – would the first two stores have helped me had I been Johnny Depp?

Yes – and there's your gap!

Having experienced some of the great personalised touchpoints Disney had to offer, it was time to take a look outside to see if Celebrity Service was alive and well elsewhere. We didn't have to wait long. Say "hello" to Nick, possibly the greatest driver in the world. During our 12-day stay, we must have ordered around 30 Uber rides to take us to and from the theme parks and shopping malls. And of all of these rides, only one stood out. Come to think of it, in my three decades of booking taxis this is the only driver to stand out.

I call in the Uber. Nick responded with a personal text, "Hey there, Geoff. I'm Nick, your Uber driver. I have your request and I'm on my way. We will see you soon, over by where the taxis and Disney buses are."

When we arrived at the collection point, he was stood ready and waiting outside the car with the trunk open ready to welcome us. He reached out and shook my hand (he actually shook my hand!) "Hi, Geoff, I am Nick. Leave all your bags and jump in the car." Moments later, he got in the driver's seat turned around to face Grace and Elliot and said, "Before we set off I have some gifts for you." Nick handed over six packs of stickers including Spiderman and Frozen pictures – we had two very happy backseat drivers.

He then asked, "What sort of music do you like?" and swiftly changed the station to play some pop music for our daughter. He then asked, "Hey, Geoff, what sort of mobile phone do you have?" An iPhone was my reply. He then pulled out a bunch of phone chargers, picked out the right one and said, "Here you are. Give yourself some juice. You'll be no doubt low since you've been in the park all day." Along our route he continued to give us helpful holiday hints and tips with a voucher for the Orlando big wheel.

This isn't a story about Uber versus Taxis. It's about Nick versus the world. Nick wins. Be like Nick!

Apart from family, I have another passion; a certain well-known and ridiculously successful film franchise (which you will have gathered by now in some of these stories).

A room had been booked at the Crowne Plaza, London The City hotel, on the eve of an event I was going to be delivering the very next day for their entire team.

So they know I am coming, and they also know about my two loves via some shrewd research on my social media channels. So what did they do? As I entered the room, the first surprise that hit me was three pairs of Star Wars socks laid out on the bed. Second surprise, a pair of R2D2 slippers by the bedside. Third surprise, a Stormtrooper speaker system. Fourth, and for me the best, was a Star Wars themed message welcoming me to the hotel.

The very first quote in this book is dedicated to my all-time favourite comic, Sir Billy Connolly. "The Queen thinks the world smells of paint." It highlights the fact that every person would go out of their way to make everything look perfect for her arrival. At this point I thought, "Ahh, but they've only done this because it's me, as I'll be talking about Celebrity Service tomorrow."

The next morning I asked, was this the case? I was wrong.

I was informed that everyone on the front desk has complete independence to look out for opportunities to do this for any guest. Hobbies, interests, special occasions can all be celebrated with a very sizeable budget set aside every month to do so. Does your team have the independence to spot opportunities to create Celebrity Service?

Dear Mr Rahul,

Welcome to our hotel. I hope you had a great journey to the hotel. I heard a whisper in the force telling me you are a fan of Star Wars please enjoy these gifts from us. As the wise Qui-Gon Jinn said 'Your focus determines your reality'.

Kind Regards

Benno.

CROWNE PLAZA
LONDON - THE CITY

19 New Bridge Street, London, EC4V 6DB, United Kingdom
+44 (0)20 7438 8000 | loncy.info@ihg.com | crowneplaza.com/londonthecity
CrownePlazaLondonCity CPLondonCity CrownePlazaLondonCity
Crowne Plaza London - The City Crowne Plaza London - The City

99

The JW Marriot Marquois Hotel in Dubai is a record breaker. It's the tallest hotel in the world, reaching to an ear popping 355 meters tall. Whilst many would find this impressive, sometimes it's the smallest of details that will make you stand out from the competition.

I entered the restaurant at 7am. The waiter showed me to my seat then asked, "Can I get you any teas or coffees, sir?"

"I'll have tea, please."

Moments later a jug of hot water arrived, along with a selection of tea bags on a side plate and then this (see below). The well-used phrase the "devil is in the detail" is certainly meant for these precise moments. Do I really need to time my cup of tea? Probably not, but is this their way of saying, everything we do here is to make everything special during your stay? Possibly so. Whatever the reason for the Perfect Tea Timer, I have only ever seen this in this particular Marriott hotel. Both independent from the competition and their own brand.

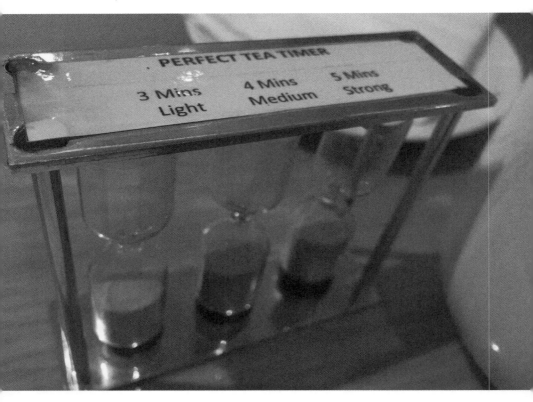

Richard Searles has worked for utility giant Northumbrian Water for over 22 years. He's a mechanical engineer by trade, and is now Customer Contact Manager.

When I heard about the level of independence their engineers and sewerage teams have alongside the call centre, I knew I just had to meet him to find out more.

He told me they have over four million customers reaching from the Scottish borders, Cumbria, Yorkshire and down to Suffolk. Of course, these are a different kind of consumer – they can't swap suppliers unless they up sticks and move. Nevertheless, Northumbrian Water is regulated by OFWAT and every quarter research is conducted to benchmark their customer service. Get it wrong and fines are there to be received! On a scale of 0–5 Richard explains, "We always aim for a 6. We know it's impossible to achieve a 6, but we may just hit the 5."

Richard explained: "At Northumbrian Water a cultural change programme called, "Our Way", includes "Our Gift To You", where, as a team, if we think we can help with a problem or see the opportunity to delight, we will take it. For example, if the company makes a mistake or leaves a mess, etc., the sewerage worker or distribution technician on site has the independence to make a decision to speak with the customer service call centre to offer a gift. But they don't just call to order the standard bottle of wine or chocolates. When they call they will share a personal observation about the customer, including if they liked fishing, or if they were celebrating an anniversary, or if there's a new baby in the house."

To help Northumbrian Water stand out from other service providers, their gifts are ordered and sent to the customer as a surprise. Books on fishing, or a hamper, or baby products are sent as a random act of service. They collaborate with a local gift company in Darlington who distribute the gifts, but what was interesting to hear – there is no financial cap on the gifts.

Every member of the team has the authority to see the opportunity to delight the customer and to send the surprise. How independent are your team and organisation? Are there rules to stop such service?

Long before I was due to work with the Red Carnation group I was asked by the Managing Director, Jonathan Raggett, to get a real feel for what they are all about. Not as an official mystery shopper, but more as an observer. What you are about to see is truly memorable...

Which Way?

The team at the Montague On The Gardens hotel knew I was coming, but they also knew why I was coming. I was staying in London as I had an event with the Royal Bank of Scotland the very next day. As I entered the room they had printed two sets of directions on how I could get to the venue. One by tube and the other by bus.

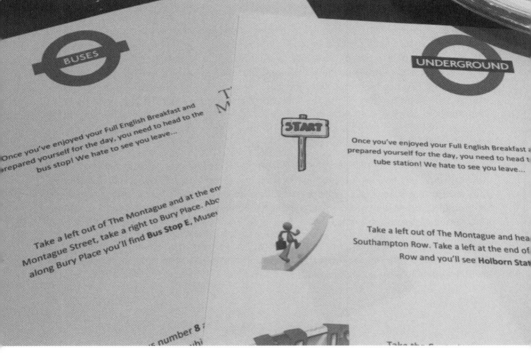

The second visit was something I've never experienced before. As I entered the room there were some handmade cupcakes with my name on them, and then a microphone (tool of the trade). But the greatest of all was a handmade lectern with notes on the place where I was delivering the next day. I repeat, the lectern was handmade! The Guest Service Manager was the one who spotted the opportunity. When I recorded the video (you can see it on YouTube) I showed this to the General Manager, who had no idea she had done this.

Have you given your team 100% independence to create memorable Celebrity Service moments?

We were so close to Buckingham Palace we could technically see the Queen watching TV. The Ramm family set off for London for a few days, holiday and we stayed at the Rubens property. They create a brilliant and exciting first impression as they have their very own children's check-in. Little ones write down the things they'd like to see and do and all of the fuss is focused on them by the staff. And then they receive a hotel passport. Inside every page they have to collect a signature from a different member of the team. Once the passport is full they win a prize! Oh, and at the back of the passport you can say who your favourite staff member was. Congratulations Stuart – Grace and Elliot loved your warm, funny and generous-with-your-time personality.

The last visit to a Red Carnation hotel was at the Milestone. Not to be outdone by their London-based colleagues, they said they knew I supported a certain team and then did this (see next page)... It's the first time I've smiled at anything remotely to do with my team in over six years.

ROARING PUBLICITY

If you wanted to respond to a disappointed customer, what would you do? Give them a freebie? Offer a future discount? Or simply put a smile on their face?

Here in the UK, Bill Bennett made a cheeky request to a customer service adviser that he wanted a drawing of a smiley dinosaur. And this was exactly what he received.

Mr Bennett then took to the internet to proudly show off the drawing, and it went viral.

The story began when he wrote to retail giants Marks & Spencer, asking for a refund after he was mistakenly charged £3.00 for a £1.90 salmon sandwich at a store in Taunton, Somerset.

He received a reply offering him a gift card, but a few weeks later it had still not arrived, so he wrote again – asking for a "hand-drawn picture of a smiley dinosaur" to compensate "for the inconvenience".

He expected his request to be ignored. But Steve Jones, a customer adviser, who seemed to share Mr Bennett's sense of humour, sent him a £5 gift card, the sketch and a note reading: "Please also find a picture of a smiling dinosaur, hand-drawn.

"Unfortunately art was never my strong point, but I hope you will appreciate it."

It's a wonderful story that social interaction can help brands reach out to a vast audience with their acts of wit, cheek or humour.

How can you demonstrate some
INDEPENDENCE
in your business?

CELEBRITY
SERVICE

The business has been done and you appreciate the fact that your customer or client chose you. You would of course thank them straight away, but take note, the "Thank You" in Celebrity Service also stands for the after care and keep-in-touch ideas that can continually delight, surprise, help, and inform.

First, ask yourself this fundamental service question – who has thanked you for your business recently? I am not talking about the "thank you" message on a receipt or a "thank you, please call again" sign. I am talking about genuine appreciation or a random act of kindness after you have made a purchase.

Attending the Paralympic Games in the Olympic Stadium in London was simply one of the greatest days out we have ever had. The Olympic stadium on the morning of Day 4 was packed with pure inspiration, so imagine my delight when I met face to face the Blade Stunner herself, Stef Reid.

I told her what an inspiration she was and that we actually saw her medal in the long jump at the Olympic Stadium. I said Grace was in awe and it was a day she'd remember for the rest of her life. Stef then said, "Thank you for coming to see us," and "What's your address? I may have a little something to send Grace."

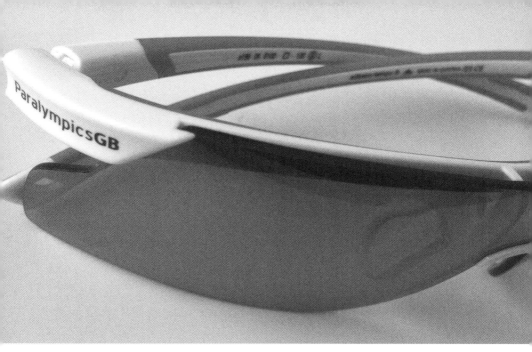

A week later, a limited edition set of Adidas Paralympic Game sunglasses arrived together with a signed note from Stef.

It may be a little easier saying thank you from one person to another, but what would you do if you were a global player in the telecoms arena?

To thank me for my business, Carphone Warehouse sent the following box, and inside was a bar of Lindt chocolate.

I've NEVER had an advertising budget, but I've always had a customer service budget!

Since I started in business back in 2002, I have re-invested the profits of my business back into my clients at Christmas time to say "Thank You" for booking me this year. Year one, I delivered six giant cookies with the words: "Wishing you sweet success this year". (Don't worry, it gets better.) Year two, I delivered over 70 potted office plants with a card reading: "Here's to continued growth for the year ahead". Year three, 151 lottery tickets were purchased and stuck inside the Christmas card saying: "Thanks a million for your business this year". (One person won £10.)

Since 2008, I have sent hundreds of large boxes of chocolates across six continents. In the first week of December, selection boxes, bars and edible novelties (and for those of you who have read OMG or seen me speak – Milk Tray) land on my clients' desks. For the first few years my phone used to light up for 48 hours after they arrived and messages saying, "OMG, Geoff, you're not going to believe what's just arrived!" Hearing the excitement in my clients' voices is just wonderful. However, of late, the phone has stopped and has been replaced by images posted onto Twitter, Facebook and Instagram.

What will you send your clients and customers to say "Thank you" for the business they have given you this year?

Tweet	Tweet

UKATA
@UKATA_Official

OMG moment from @GeoffRamm thank you for treating the UKATA Team today! It was great to have you at our AGM ow.ly/mmL9306FwIA

Younique_yudi
@YouniqueYudi

A fantastic surprise this morning in the post #myfav #omg. Now this is brilliant customer service. Thank you 🎄🎄🎄 @GeoffRamm

Mila Hardware
@milahardware_uk

OMG! You know its Christmas when your Wednesday starts like this! @geofframm you've made us smile from ear to ear! Thanks! #CelebrityService

Reply to Mila Hardware

Eve-Anne McCarron
@EveAnneMcCarron

Not a bad thing to arrive into office to see!!! Thanks from all the crew here @GeoffRamm #celebrityservice

Reply to Eve-Anne McCarron

Home   Notifications   Moments   Messages   Me

Michelle Andrade ▶ **Geoff Ramm**
December 16, 2014 ·

We can for sure tell that it has been one of the nicest and coolest surprises ever 😊 thank you so much for being such an awesome person and sending this amazing gift to all of us. We send you a big hug and we look forward to see you again soon. Merry Christmas 🎅 — with Andrea Mendoza Ojeda and Meche Mogollón.

Like · Comment · Stop Notifications · Share

👍 Hayley Ramm, Dean Lindsay, Michelle Masters and 16 others like this.

💬 View 2 more comments

Andrea Mendoza Ojeda Jessica Thomson y Andrea Andre Herrera vengan mañana a la ofic para comer los chocolates 😊
See Translation
December 16, 2014 at 7:12pm · Like · 👍 1

Andre Herrera Claro que Mañana estoy ahi! me avisan a que hora 😊 q hermoso regalo!!!! ya lloro con la foto! jaja
See Translation
December 16, 2014 at 7:16pm · Like

Andrea Mendoza Ojeda ven tipo 1 pm para ir a almorzar 😊
See Translation
December 16, 2014 at 7:16pm · Like

Andre Herrera perfecto! mañana nos vemos chicas! eeeeeee!!!
See Translation
December 16, 2014 at 7:19pm · Like · 👍 1

Geoff Ramm Ahhh delighted they arrived in time, best wishes Santa Ramm.
December 16, 2014 at 7:55pm · Like · 👍 5

Gabriela Falconi Jaramillo Que Lindas todas!
December 16, 2014 at 7:58pm · Like · 👍 3

Write a comment...

Take every opportunity to say

THANK YOU.

CELEBRITY
SERVICE

Philadelphia... it was midweek, and outside the streets were being pounded by heavy rain as we ventured out for a meal and a few drinks. Around half of the restaurants were closed, and the ones that were open were sparse, to say the least.

All except one: The Walnut Street Supper Club. Inside, it was packed to the rafters, bustling with atmosphere, and we were fortunate to be given a table right in front of a small stage and piano.

Whilst we were ordering drinks, the pianist jumped onto the stage, sat down, and called out one of the singer's names. She hurriedly ran to the stage and proceeded to belt out a flawless song.

Another singer got up five minutes later, and then another. What I found incredible was that these were not professional entertainers. They certainly didn't look like entertainers.

They were the waitresses and waiters. Whilst not serving, they each sang their hearts out to the customers. It was a brilliant night in which I saw a full team working as one to deliver exceptional service.

By 11:30pm there were just four of us left – myself and my good friends, Corey Perlman, David Newman, and Jay Baer. As the last ones standing, we were treated to an encore by all of the staff.

It wouldn't have mattered had we been Tom Cruise, George Clooney, Brad Pitt and Johnny Depp; they brilliantly delivered Celebrity Service and we loved it. We spoke about it, and, as you can see, I wrote about it.

Why should it just be your service department that delivers service? Celebrity Service flows through everyone, from CEO to office junior, from Managing Director to the lavatory cleaner. Watch the video on my YouTube channel to see the final encore from that great night!

15th June, 2014 and a wonderful surprise gift on Father's Day... James Bond, Jack Bauer, Jason Bourne, eat your heart out... I was going to become a stunt driver for the day!

We all travelled down to the family-run business Stunt Drive Experience in Stockton, where I was to learn how to donut a BMW Z3, and hand-brake turn and parallel park a Mini at high speed.

As we entered the cabin to hand over our gift vouchers and sign in, we were welcomed by a lovely lady, Jane Bird. Along with another 13 drivers with their partners and children, there must have been 30 plus people helping themselves to tea, coffee, biscuits, and squash. Once everyone had signed in, we walked outside to the stunt driving briefing, led by Paul Bird – one of the most charismatic and quick-witted people you are ever likely to meet.

He was joined by his daughter, Kelly Bird, Sarah Hall and Brian Jukes. All four of them gave the safety briefing, and then did something pretty special...

They asked everyone, including the non-drivers, to say their name and introduce themselves to the rest of the group. So we did. After each person, the Stunt Drive team would all shout out, "Hello, [person's name]," all the way around the circle. We got round the whole group, and then it happened. They announced that they were going to go around the group and remember every person's name. And they did! Everyone was amazed, everyone felt special, and it set the tone for the next few hours.

Remembering someone's name is one thing, but 30 in a row? That is something special, and is just one of the ways in which they deliver Celebrity Service.

They say leave the best til last... and the best for me is simply proof that the Celebrity Service technique works. It can inspire, it can galvanise the team, and it will create the gap in customer service the competition can't touch...

It all happened on the wonderful Mediterranean island of Malta. EC English Language Centres is a very successful business, which prides itself on having high levels of customer service and positive feedback from their pupils and agents.

They teach English to over 40,000 pupils a year in their 18 schools throughout the USA, Canada, UK, Malta and South Africa.

On the 8th April they asked me to speak at their Senior Leaders and Marketers Conference, to help further inspire their customer service thinking and delivery.

On arrival, I was met at the airport at 1:00am by the taxi driver, Nunzio (below). On the journey to the hotel, I found out that he'd worked with EC since they began in 1991.

He was knowledgeable, friendly, but, most of all, passionate. He is the person the pupils meet for the very first time when they travel from all over the world to study English in Malta.

It was a wonderful few days working with the team, and by the end everyone was whipped up to thinking differently whilst upgrading every touchpoint to a Celebrity Service standard.

I certainly wasn't expecting a call just one month later from EC asking me to come back to Malta, this time to deliver a keynote and interactive workshop for their admissions and sales teams. I touched down at 2:30am on Friday 6th June. Nunzio was not there this time, but a colleague was, along with a very impressive sign which was waiting for me...

A VERY WARM WELCOME TO MALTA, GEOFF RAMM!
From The EC Sales Team ☺

In just six weeks, EC had designed a brand-new welcome sign by upgrading from the simple display of a corporate logo to a montage of photos of their teams in Malta, as well as a personalised message at the bottom.

At 2:50am I was met by Alexander at the desk at the Valentina hotel in St Julians. "Before I check you in, I just want to welcome you to the hotel," and then he reached out his hand and shook mine! Now there's a first. Having looked on TripAdvisor I noticed they were number one – I said I was looking forward to staying at the #1 rated hotel in Malta... his reply: "Ah yes, we are number one right now but we must always keep pushing!"

My room was on the fourth floor. After a delayed flight, and with an early start the next morning, I needed to hit the pillow, fast! But not tonight. As I walked in, I was met by constant surprises!

Orange (EC branded colours) balloons were at the foot of the bed, and a pair of "I Love Malta" flip flops sat beneath them.

On the bed was an orange (of course) towel, a nursery rhymes book, and an orange glass ornament in the shape of a snail, hidden underneath the pages of the book. Beside the desk area and alarm clock was a box of Yorkshire Tea, biscuits, sweets, chilled drinks, fruit, a chicken and mushroom Pot Noodle, and further chilled drinks in the fridge!

I filmed the experience and posted to YouTube – type in Geoff Ramm Celebrity Service EC English Language Schools to watch.

Now every pupil who chooses EC receives a personalised welcome board and gifts galore in their rooms when they arrive.

This was a celebrity welcome which took just a matter of weeks to permeate throughout the team, and one which will continue to raise the bar and help them to stand out from the competition.

They understand the concept, they bought into the idea, and are creating ideas they never previously thought of.

How can you improve

YOU AND YOUR TEAM?

TELL THE TRUTH

ANSWER, TRUTHFULLY, THE FOLLOWING QUESTIONS:

Proposals:

Q. A potential client has asked for a proposal from you. How long does it take you to write and send it?

A. A day, week or longer?

Q. How would you deliver that proposal?

A. By email (saved as a pdf), by second or first class post, or express courier?

NOW LET'S INTRODUCE "CELEBRITY SERVICE"...

Angelina Jolie asks for a proposal from you...

Q. How long does it now take to deliver that proposal?

A. My guess is her proposal will have made it to the top of the pile, sitting in front of everyone else's. Possibly everything in your office or workshop will stop until it is done.

Q. How would you deliver it?

A. I think you can forget about emailing or using a postbox. If it's possible, I'd place my bets that you would deliver it by hand. It would be printed on the best paper you could lay your hands on, and quite possibly your car would be cleaned en route to accentuate the wonderful suit or dress you were wearing.

The simple concept of a Celebrity Service proposal would make a big impact on every one of your customers. So what will you do, starting from today, to raise your client care to Celebrity Service?

Your business is closing for the day.

Before the shutters come down the phone rings. You let it go to answer machine, and hear that the customer has a problem.

Q. Do you rush back to pick up the call to help? Do you visit that customer to help put the problem right? Or do you wait until the morning to call back?

Q. Johnny Depp leaves the message. Do you do the same as above? Or do you pick up and go straight round to fix the problem?

HOW TO USE

FOUR COLUMNS for you and your team to discuss, debate, and improve upon every customer service touchpoint to help take you from good to celebrity...

TOUCHPOINT	CURRENT SERVICE

CELEBRITY SERVICE

If you are struggling to think of an A-list movie hunk or goddess then there are a few to help you on the next page...

CELEBRITY NAME	IMPROVED SERVICE

LAW FREEMAN
BALE
WATSON
ANNISTON STALLONE
FERRELL
DAYLEWIS JACKMAN
WASHINGTON BERRY
BLOOM AFFLECK
ROBERTS JACKSON
HOPKINS
DE NIRO STREEP
CARREY

HOW TO EXCEL IN YOUR BUSINESS USING CELEBRITY SERVICE

You get the simple yet effective method of Celebrity Service, but how will others in your department or business adopt this way of thinking?

You will need: celeb magazine, glue, scissors and picture frame

Step One:

Each staff member of the department chooses their own Celebrity Hunk or Goddess. They print them out, cut them out, and they frame them to their heart's content.

Step Two:

Everyone strategically places the image near to them when they are connecting with the customer, e.g. by the telephone, computer, reception desk, staff room, locker or in their vehicle.

Step Three:

After every interaction, a glance to the image is enough to make everyone think… if this was this person, what would I do?

What they are creating is a visual reminder of the person they need to think of before every email, face-to-face or social media touchpoint to help them scale greater heights when needing to outserve the competition.

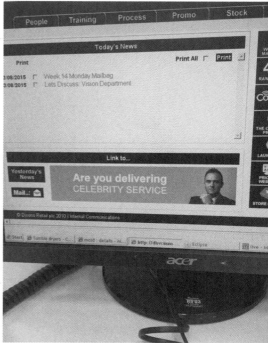

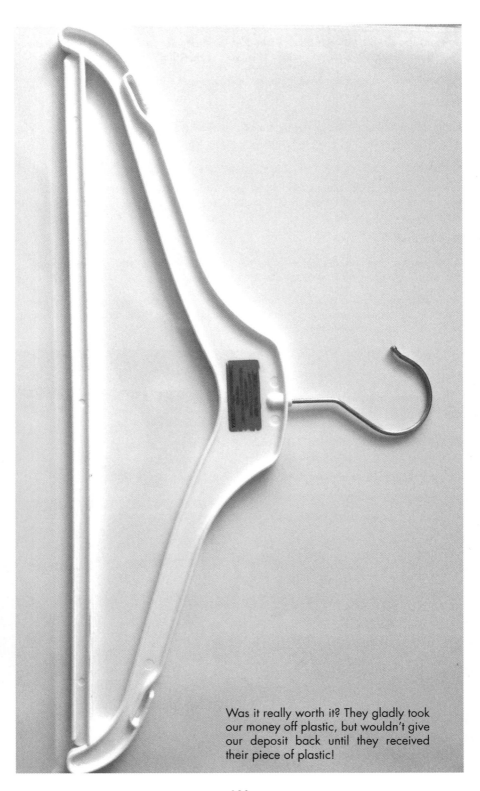

Was it really worth it? They gladly took our money off plastic, but wouldn't give our deposit back until they received their piece of plastic!

N-ICE EXPERIENCE: 120 CHALLENGE

And here it is...

The incredible hand-carved rose made out of the three flavours I ordered from the Amorino ice-cream brand. Of course, you can still have your regular scoop or tub, but everyone in the queue that day ordered the more expensive floral design. The server used a knife and delicately handmade each petal to create this masterpiece.

What ideas did you create to make it a memorable third option...

THE RESULTS ARE IN

VROOM FOR AN AWARD (OR TWO)

So if Celebrity Service is the philosophy, the technique and the ground-breaking system to outperform the competition, and the stories and illustrations in this book bring it to life, then there can only be one thing left to reveal. The results.

Over the years, I've worked with some of the most iconic brands in the world, as well as some of the amazing entrepreneurial clients. Over time, I'd receive the results of the changes they have made as a result of our engagement. The news may filter in from social media, an email or one of those pre-historic phone call things. But when I hear or read what has happened I am beyond delighted.

Moto Direct: Remember them? They built bike-fit especially for the customers to sit on so they could measure and calculate the right bike for the customer. The managing director, Terry Birtles, actually sent me a video (which can be viewed on my YouTube channel). He explains what they did as a result of adopting Celebrity Service into their culture including meeting and greeting clients at airports, private transfers and gifts already in the bedrooms as they arrived.

The result? They won the Motorcycle News "Wholesaler Of The Year" Award (see below). Terry added, "For us, we talk about Celebrity Service at each opportunity we have to interact with our partners and consumers – we recently won distribution of a Japanese car racing helmet brand and part of our approach was to have welcome letters and gifts translated into Japanese and our presentations and welcome boards were dual language. The distributor of the year award was without doubt helped by the way we looked for ways to be different and ways to add something that was unexpected."

MAKING BEDS & MAKING HISTORY

The Crowne Plaza, Kensington is a stunning 5-star hotel in the heart of London. After two half days of sharing the philosophy and ideas with everyone from the chef to the concierge and the cleaners to the bar staff, everyone who attended went on to create a piece of hotel history.

The General Manager, Edward Bracken sent me the following email:

Geoff, we are having an amazing start to the year – just finished our best financial month on record with the highest service metrics cumulatively for the first 6 months, and the highest levels in my 4 years here. When I took on this business my customer satisfaction was 84%. It has been a huge task to get to 86.4%. Now running at 88.49% is outstanding and puts us up in the top performers.

So I am a believer!

The team has really embraced Celebrity Service initiatives. Let me know if you are coming to London and we can look after you.

Let's catch up soon.

Edward

TOP MARKS

EC English Language Schools: after the two amazing trips to Malta, EC took onboard every aspect of Celebrity Service but then they added their own twist called "Orange Carpet Service". It's a story I love to tell in my talks and the very last email I received at the end of 2016 was from Michelle Falzon at EC which said: "Hi, Geoff, thought you might like to see this!"

They had only gone and WON a UK Customer Experience Award for Design & Improvement.

BEN TEN

"At our Annual Fraser's Hospitality General Managers Forum (last year in Frankfurt, Germany), we were lucky enough to spend one of the days listening to customer service and marketing speaker/extraordinaire Geoff Ramm. He was infectious, hilarious, engaging, eye opening, mind-blowing and perhaps, above all, simple, real and relevant.

He introduced his concept of Celebrity Service – the nuts and bolts being, that despite all your best efforts to treat every guest as equally important and every single arrival as a VIP, that if Brad Pitt or George Clooney (for example) were to make a booking at your hotel, you would invariably do a variety of things differently, and indeed go above and beyond, what you would do for all your other "VIP Guests"... confirming the service they received, is actually above what you would normally deliver, given they have that celebrity factor!

On the 12th June 2007, prior to our hotel's official opening, and many years prior to my arrival at the Fraser Suites Sydney, our Front Office Team accepted a walk-in guest, literally stepping straight in from Kent Street and asking for a room. For the sake of this story, let's call this guest, Mr Ross.

Unbeknown to us at the time, Mr Ross stayed 225 consecutive nights on that visit and a few weeks ago, Mr Ross, my most regular and favourite guest, celebrated staying at our property, on and off each and every week for a total of 10 years. You could say, in our eyes, Mr Ross is a celebrity.

In this instance, I asked my team if we could trial Geoff Ramm's concept of "Celebrity Service" on Mr Ross in the coming weeks, to celebrate his 10-year milestone. As Mr Ross returned to the hotel, following the long weekend on Tuesday 13th June 2017, our team prepared his suite as we always do... delivering the items he stores with us each week and setting them up in his suite specifically how he likes them, hanging up his suits and freshly-pressed shirts ready for the week ahead, preparing his favourite arrival amenity including certain types of fruit and his staple sparkling mineral water – and we write a card each week with a different and often quirky message (same generic card each and every week – how boring!)... only this time, given the occasion, my team decided to fill his entire suite with helium balloons, and also the oversized "10" balloons.

As he sifted through the sea of balloons on his arrival, we placed a small model helicopter on his table next to the fruit, sparkling mineral water and card... and on the Welcome Card this week, the team had written...

"Mr Ross, thanks for the last 10 years, and here's to the next 10 at Fraser Suites Sydney! We've taken the liberty of arranging Helicopter Flights over Sydney Harbour for you and your wife the next time she accompanies you, although if she's not keen, I'm pretty sure Ben is happy to go with you! All the best, and many thanks for your continued support, from the team at Fraser Suites Sydney.

"I consider two important lessons learnt following Mr Ross' milestone, being that one, with the almost infinite ways to book a hotel room via various distribution channels, a walk-in guest, if managed correctly can become a brand ambassador and loyal customer for life (well, 10 years anyway!), so your team's knowledge and understanding of their potential impact is critical to success. And two, human connection, forming relationships and engaging with our guests is the cornerstone to real hospitality and running successful hotels, the importance of which, often cannot be measured.

"I guess following this example, at Fraser Suites Sydney, our new vision as I write this is short, sharp and simple: 'Deliver Celebrity Service to each and every guest.' The difficulty being, that it is easy to deliver Celebrity Service to Mr Ross, as we know everything about him... the harder part being, how do we deliver Celebrity Service to the next guest who walks through the front doors...

"I'm heading off to the Lobby now to welcome the next guest, I'll let you know how we go..."

Ben Nesbitt, General Manager, Frasers Hospitality, Sydney, Australia

KEEPING UP WITH THE KARDASHIANS

Whilst speaking at the Goldwell conference in Shanghai, I challenged the salon owner managers to upgrade their current level of service to Celebrity Status. Imagine my surprise when I received this email from Wildlife Hair Company who had taken Celebrity Service one stage further... Enjoy!

Dear Geoff,

My wife Jayne and I were at the Goldwell seminar you spoke at in Shanghai and had a blast. We both liked your Celebrity Service section and thought we should bring it back to our team. Rather than just re-tell your story we decided to put it into play "for real". We have a monthly joint staff meeting for our two salons with approx 30 staff at the meeting. Kim Kardashian is doing a tour of Australia and next week she has an appearance at Westfield Shopping Centre. Our staff were all aware of the trip and one had even entered a competition to meet her. I told them that we had been asked to do the hair for Kim and her entourage as she hated getting her hair done in a hotel room and our salon has wonderful views of Sydney harbour and the bridge. At this point I had one young member of staff ask me if I was joking, "Do I look like I am joking?" I answered and she had to leave the room to "compose" herself. I then listed the conditions on our PowerPoint big screen:

- **5am start**
- **Everybody has to wear white**
- **Only Kanye music to be played**
- **Fresh flowers and fruit**
- **No talking to Kim or her entourage**
- **Top secret so no social media, etc.**

I had half the staff put their hands up to be there at 5am dressed in white, another two were putting together a Kanye playlist and someone was going to the markets for fruit and flowers on the way to work.

Point made.

Thanks for the idea.

Gary and Jayne

Wild Life Hair, Sydney, Australia

www.wildlifehair.com

HEADING FOR THE TOP

Google "The Headland" in Cornwall and you will discover a picture perfect setting on the North Cornish coast. Concurrent years of Celebrity Service for the entire team in 2017 and 2018 saw within the space of just 12 months the concepts and ideas you've already read so far in this book being engrained into the behaviours of The Headland team to deliver exceptional service for every guest, every time. Here is just a snapshot of a few of the things they did as a result of the very first day:

- Stamped blank postcards for children to send to a loved one back home.
- Luggage tags which are sent home with guests' lost property, saying: "I have enjoyed my extended stay but I am ready to come home now".
- Little Headlander badges, bathrobes and stickers.
- Biodegradable straws in the bar – no more plastic!
- Key cards saying: "Welcome home".
- The autonomy for every team member to arrange a special gift or gesture if they know it will enhance their stay.

And it doesn't stop there. Literally hours after the second Celebrity Service event, the team attended the Cornwall Business Awards... and this was the result:

On Thursday 19th April, we were presented with the prestigious Customer Focus Award, highlighting our continued commitment to treating every guest like a "VIP". On the evening, judges described the Headland as, "An iconic business that sets the standard for customer service in the hospitality sector." The praise continued, "In all parts of their business, The Headland continues to innovate and develop new ways of delighting customers." The judges said they were particularly impressed with the language used by the hotel, choosing not to refer to "Customer Service" but instead the "celebrity service" they provide – treating each customer as they would an A-list Hollywood star.

The Cornwall Business Awards' recognition follows gold wins at both the South West and Cornwall Tourism Awards – both for recognition in Customer Service.

Lucy Brigden, Guest Relations Manager

WHO IS YOUR HIGH FLYER?

Remember Christina? The best cabin crew member of all time.

Well, the following day I was invited back into the studio at Radio 702 in Johannesburg. And strangely enough, as well as going out live across the airwaves, the interview was also recorded on camera and uploaded to YouTube. During the show I regaled the story and praised every touchpoint. Now at this point I never knew her full name (asking a stranger for their photograph as well as their full name is just not protocol is it?)

Six months later Christina contacted me completely out of the blue via Facebook. A friend of hers who was a pilot on another airline came across the footage and sent it to her. Christina's message started with, "Hi, Geoff, you'll not remember me..." OMG! Oh yes I do – I mention you at just about every talk I do!

We became Facebook friends and have stayed in touch ever since. Three years on from that experience, littered with excitement, I was presenting at the Customer Experience World event in Johannesburg. I told everyone that day about the story and then for the finale I said, "And she's here today." There was a sharp intake of breath from everyone in the room as Christina stood up and waved to everyone. That was such a cool moment.

"Who's the Christina in your business?" This has somewhat become a verb or a motto with many of my clients.

EXCITEMENT

...member of cabin crew
... flights you've ever
..., but more
... of publicity has
... given to the wonderful
... board South West Airlines in
the United States, and by now, like me,
you've probably watched many viral
videos they have featured in.
There was no video camera to capture
this trip, but what I am about to share
with you is quite simply the greatest
cabin crew member of all time.

She brought excitement to the
passengers in just 90 minutes.

I'd just finished speaking at a
conference in Harare, Zimbabwe.
Having arrived at the airport, I quickly
received my boarding card.

Glancing at it I was mildly excited to see
I was sat in 1F. I'd been upgraded! (I
was wearing my 3 piece suit after all).

Now, I have a lot more confidence in
larger planes than I do smaller ones.
We were called to our gate and walked
onto the tarmac. But there was no plane
to be seen, only a tiny aircraft with
propellers in the distance. Yes, this was
our plane. On the horizon, huge black
clouds started to engulf the city and the
sounds of rumbling thunder and the odd
fork lightning flash lit up the skies. I was
becoming nervous thinking by the time
we board the plane the storm would be
upon us. I walked up the stairs and was
met by two cabin crew.
"Good afternoon, sir, can we see you
boarding card?"
"Yes, certainly" (but I could not find which
pocket in my suit I'd put it in).
"Oh, we do apologise Sir."
"No that's okay, here it is".
She paused, looking at my upgraded
ticket, and then she lent in and
whispered...
"Oh... you have won a prize!"
"What have I won?"
"I can't tell you now, but I will soon".
I walked a few short steps and took...

my seat beside an older gentleman (the
propelled plane was so small we were in
Economy!). I turned to the gentleman and
said:
"Did you win a prize?"
"Yes, but she wouldn't tell me what it was."
At this point the row across the aisle turned
to us and said that they had also been told
they were prize winners.

Being sat at the front gave me a great
vantage point as I could hear every single
conservation as the rest of the passengers
boarded. What struck me was that
everyone received a compliment, and I
mean everyone. Whether it was about
their clothes, hair or even about the toys
being carried by children as they boarded
with their parents.

Everyone was buckled in and we started to
taxi. The cabin crew member then picked
up the phone and announced to everyone
that she was delighted everyone was on
board and then proceeded to say – "And
you have the best looking cabin crew
serving you today", with a sarcastic smile.

She asked very politely if everyone would
take out of their front pockets the safety
instructions and read them, as it would
really help us all should an incident occur.

HEROES OR VILLAINS

BAD SANTA

Take for example this Santa's Grotto in an out-of-town retail outlet that should have been serving to entice, encourage and deliver a great experience. Instead, they littered their communications with the most vile and negative wording for parents paying good money.

NO PHOTOGRAPHY ALLOWED

Warning to parents!
Please note you only get 1 chance at a photograph.
No retakes. Thank You

EMIRATES EXCELLENCE

Now here's a wonderful piece of celebrity thinking just for parents.

To assist carrying tired children all the way to the passport desk and baggage carousel, Emirates Airline have placed strollers/buggies all over the airport for families to use. They are FREE too!. How amazing is that?

You can also watch this example on my YouTube channel... enjoy!

ALL YOU CAN'T EAT

This was the biggest sign on the window of this restaurant...
Is it any wonder businesses struggle?

• COMPANY POLICY

Due to our company policy we regret that all customers coming into the restaurant will be charged for the buffet whether they have anything from the buffet or not. Sorry for any inconvenience this may cause.

• The Management

EGG ON YOUR FACE

To anyone visiting the Premier Inn "Centurion" Hotel in Tamworth, I can whole-heartedly recommend ordering the soft-boiled eggs.

As you can see, the chefs draw smiley faces on every egg that leaves the kitchen. Simple and effective.

A QUICK DIP IN THE POO

You can have an Olympic-sized swimming pool, but attention to detail will leave you drowning with the rest.

ON YOUR BIKE

Lovers of two wheeler vehicles simply love Moto Direct. Their motorbike brand RST is famous throughout the world for their high-quality clothing and equipment, including pads, jackets and helmets. At their headquarters in Chesterfield, they also have a showroom which includes road and push bikes.

Go into any bike store and you'll see the one you like, sit on it, adjust the handlebars and seat so it's comfortable before making the purchase. But at Moto Direct they'll not take your money until you sit on the static bike-fit below. This machine will record the best seating position for your height and weight and will therefore recommend the best bike for you. This attention to detail to ensure the rider gets the best fit is just one of the reasons they are so sought after.

THE WALK OF SHAME

And this is how I was welcomed into a hotel recently...

WE ASK GUESTS TO

KINDLY REMOVE

THEIR SHOES

BEFORE WALKING

UP THE STAIRS

THANK YOU

ASPECTS OF LOVE

Imagine that you had hurt your back and had to postpone your holiday by a fortnight. You call the holiday company to hopefully re-arrange and they do so brilliantly.

Now imagine the people you had booked with had seen you talk about Celebrity Service. They remembered listening to the story of Uber Nick and that your daughter loves to listen to Little Mix. And also that your son adores Star Wars.

The image on the next page was taken as we entered the Fistral Beach Apartment in Newquay. The amazing team at Aspects Holidays had created this truly unique, personalised welcome pack.

Grace screamed with delight whilst Elliot grabbed the Star Wars games compendium and, of course, Hayley and I chilled the bottle of Prosecco whilst I used the heat pads on my back.

Again, when you know a piece of information about your customer, don't be shy in using it. Use the Two-Minute Challenge and create something memorable.

This is how Grace is welcomed into the Hamleys toy store in London. How do you welcome your customers as they enter your business?

THE END

FOR NOW?

So there you have it, from singing waitresses, to the greatest cabin crew in the skies, a bicycle pump which stays up all night just for you, to the personalised video of a car you are thinking of buying, Celebrity Service can stop you in your tracks at any time, leaving you with the greatest feeling for that person and that brand.

It will forever be the person delivering Celebrity Service who drives the brand, and never the brand driving the Celebrity Service experience.

What will you improve from today? 10 out of 10 is just the starting block to propel your service to another level; that level is where you will find the gap you never realised existed.

WISHING YOU EVERY
FUTURE SUCCESS.

To book Geoff for your next conference or to watch more Celebrity Service moments,

Email: geoff@geofframm.com • Website: geofframm.com • YouTube: Geoff Ramm